CHAPMAN

KNOTS
FOR BOATERS

CHAPMAN

KNOTS
FOR BOATERS

BRION TOSS
ILLUSTRATED BY GAE PILON

HEARST BOOKS
A division of Sterling Publishing Co., Inc.

New York / London
www.sterlingpublishing.com

Copyright © 1990 by Brion Toss and Hearst Communications, Inc.

This book was previously published under the title
A Chapman Nautical Guide: Knots.

Book design by Mary Moriarty
Edited by Lucy A. O'Brien
Produced by Smallwood & Stewart, New York City

Cover design by Chris Thompson.

Library of Congress Cataloging-in-Publication Data available.

10 9 8 7 6 5 4 3 2

Published by Hearst Books
A division of Sterling Publishing Co., Inc.
387 Park Avenue South, New York, N.Y. 10016

CHAPMAN and CHAPMAN PILOTING and Hearst Books
are trademarks owned by Hearst Communications, Inc.

For information about custom editions, special sales, premium and
corporate purchases, please contact Sterling Special Sales Department
at 800-805-5489 or specialsales@sterlingpublishing.com.

Distributed in Canada by Sterling Publishing
c/o Canadian Manda Group, 165 Dufferin Street
Toronto, Ontario, Canada M6K 3H6

Distributed in Australia by Capricorn Link (Australia) Pty. Ltd.
P.O. Box 704, Windsor, NSW 2756 Australia

Printed in the United States of America

Sterling ISBN 978-1-58816-778-1

CONTENTS

Acknowledgements

Most of the knots in this book are old, even ancient; we all owe thanks to those of you who, through the centuries, have invented, refined, and passed knots on for us to use.

As for the production of this book, I owe thanks to: Lucy O'Brien, my incomparable editor; to her boss, John Smallwood, for assigning this book to her; and to Hearst's Connie Roosevelt for hiring John Smallwood, after getting this project going in the first place. Civilization is great when it works.

Special thanks to the members of the International Guild of Knot Tyers (I.G.K.T). By personal action, and with articles in the Guild journal, Knotting Matters, members continue to demonstrate that knotting is a vital, valuable tradition.

FOREWORD

When I first saw Brion Toss, he was performing rope tricks in the editor's office at *Sail Magazine*. He had the technique and the banter of an accomplished street performer, but it was obvious that he also cared about his subject, and approached it seriously, even reverently.

Brion probably knows more knots and their stories than anyone since Clifford Ashley. Yet Brion's deep respect for traditional ways and materials doesn't prevent his meeting contemporary needs. In fact, he fulfills them daily, as a professional rigger.

Day-to-day needs are what this book is about. Brion encourages developing a personl repertory—it needn't be large—from which an appropriate knot can be pulled for any job that might come up. To that end, each knot's purpose is described and its differences from related knots are noted. The how-to presentation is invitingly simple.

Beyond knot-tying there are practical tips on safe winching, proper tack set-ups, and rope-end whipping.

I could make great predictions and favorable comparisons with the other, already successful, book bearing the Chapman name. Instead, I suggest you read the introduction to this volume. As Brion says, you will quickly "know more about the underlying principles of rope and ropework than most people." And you'll want to start tying knots.

Freeman Pittman
Senior Editor
Sail Magazine
(1982-1996)

CHAPTER ONE

INTRODUCTION

The most important thing to remember about knots is that every one of them developed in response to particular needs. Context, scale, purpose, and materials combine to call for an appropriate knot. No one simply invented the Bowline, for instance; there is a universal need for an easily tied, secure, jam-resistant Loop Knot, and the Bowline evolved to fill the bill.

If you dive into this book intent on memorizing knots, you will have a prodigious and largely meaningless exercise ahead of you. But if you stop and think about the particular needs that knots respond to, you will find yourself joining in the response, comprehending why knots are structured the way they are, and thus able to tie them naturally. You will see knots as elegant, highly evolved tools.

All knots are not created equal. Out of thousands of possible knots, only a handful are sufficiently versatile, trustworthy, and easily understood to be generally useful. And out of that handful an even smaller number of "core" knots are the ones you will use for the great majority of your work with rope. Learn these core knots, and you will have learned the knots you will tie 90 percent of the time or more.

The non-core knots are far from obscure. They're specialized tools for circumstances in which nothing else will do. Many of them are variations on the core knots, so you "learn one, get one free" when you're building your knot vocabulary.

Before you start studying, think about what you need to know. If you have a powerboat, you'll be most interested in mooring lines, anchor rodes, and block and tackle (for hoisting and lowering the dinghy). Start with the knots designed for your needs, choosing your own personal group of core knots. Once familiar with them, you can branch out in confidence. If you have a sailboat, you have a lot more strings to play with, but not that many more basic structures. Focus on the essentials, and the intimidating details will take care of themselves.

This is a book of knots, not of rigging. When you put your knots to work, you need to understand more than the technique of tying them and the general circumstances they suit. You need to understand the physical properties of the rope you're using, what its strengths and limitations are, and whether or not it can safely bear the load you expect it to. Knots and lines at work are often under tons of tension; a failure can have fatal consequences. There are charts at the back of this book to familiarize you with rope properties and to provide guidelines for common applications.

But if you are working on an *un*common application, or if you just don't feel confident about what you're doing, *get more information*. Consult the bibliography in this book, consult a professional rigger or sail maker, seek out friends and neighbors with successful experience with similar situations, and consult rope manufacturers.

A knot is a picky thing; if you don't tie it exactly right, it is an entirely different knot—or it is nothing at all. Pay attention to all the details in the text, illustrations, and captions, to make sure you're tying what you mean to. And always take the time to draw up (tighten) your knots so that they're stable and don't "capsize" (distort) into something else when the load comes on.

All the illustrations in this book are made from the tier's perspective. Most are shown the way a right-hander would tie them. But you will find that your retention is much better if you practice them both left- and right-handed. And your ambidexterity will come in handy out in the real world, where situations don't always favor right-handedness. Wherever possible, the text is written without reference to left or right, to make ambidextrous learning easier and to lessen confusion for us left-handers.

The best way to master a knot is to use it. Get yourself a six-foot piece of one-eighth- to one-quarter-inch-diameter rope and carry it around with you. I can guarantee that you will find opportunities to use it for practical applications (trunk tie-down, light lashing, sling, impromptu leash, etc.). And you'll always have the material to practice your core knots at odd moments.

Every art has its jargon, and knotting is no exception. But most knots are very simple things, with terms to match. To start with, knots are tied in rope. Once a piece of rope has been cut to length, knotted, and put to work, it generally becomes a *line*. A *halyard* is a line that picks things up, for example.

There are two basic constructions of rope in general use: three-strand and double-braid. Three-strand is made of three individual pieces of rope twisted evenly together. Each strand comprises a number of small- er pieces called *yarns*, and each yarn is in turn made up of *fibers*. If the fibers run the full length of the rope, the rope is described as a filament construction. If the fibers are a series of short pieces spun together, the rope is spun. Spun rope is softer and fuzzier than filament rope, so it is more comfortable to handle. However, it is slightly more elastic than filament rope, a drawback when steady tension is desired, as for halyards.

Virtually all three-strand rope available today is *right-laid* (below).

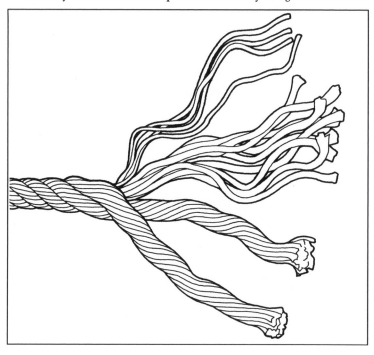

That is, the strands are twisted together so that they spiral off to the right as you sight down the length of the rope. The strands themselves are *left-laid*. This balances the rope so it is less liable to twist in use.

Double-braid rope (opposite) is just that—a braided core-tube running inside a braided cover-tube. Double-braid is less elastic and stronger for

for its size than three-strand. It's also more expensive and trickier to splice. Double-braid is available in filament and spun constructions.

Until the recent past, rope was made exclusively of natural fibers, especially hemp, Manila hemp, and flax. These have been almost entirely superseded by synthetic fibers such as Dacron™ and nylon.

Synthetics have much higher breaking strengths than natural fibers, resist deterioration well, and can be designed to suit specific jobs. High-strength, low-stretch Dacron, for instance, is good for halyards, while high-strength, high-stretch nylon is used for mooring lines, safety tethers, and other situations in which "give" is desirable, to avoid abrupt jerking motions.

Along with their advantages, modern synthetic ropes have some disadvantages. Because synthetics are so much stronger than natural fibers, they allow much higher loads on fewer pieces of rigging, so the consequence of a line breaking can be more dramatic than in times past.

But the biggest problem with synthetics is that they are slippery. Knots hold together because of friction—the less friction, the less secure the knot is. A lot of knots that have worked fine for centuries are untrustworthy when tied in slick synthetics, particularly braided filament constructions, and nylon in any construction. Knotting literature has in general been slow to respond to this problem, but there are simple, field-tested remedies. You will find that slickness compensation is a recurrent theme in the following pages.

The easiest way to learn a knot is to think of it as a series of parts arranged in a particular way. A few parts, in various combinations, make up most knots.

The first part is the *end*. You thread, pass, and tuck it around and through other parts to form knots.

Then there's the *standing part*, the inert bulk of the line that the end acts on. But you can also make other parts out of the standing part. For instance, this is a *turn* (below, top left). If you can make a turn around an

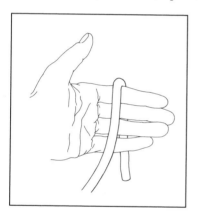

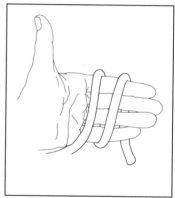

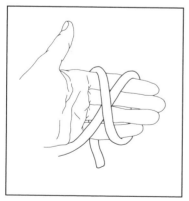

object and secure the end, you can put the line to work.

If you expect a particularly heavy load or are passing a large line around a small object or want to generate more friction for control and security, make a *round turn* (above, right). A round turn distributes pressure over a greater area than a turn, so the line can take a heavier strain without chafing on the bearing point. A round turn can also reduce strain on the knot you tie beyond it, making that knot less likely to "jam" (tighten up so much that it becomes difficult to untie). Some knots start with a *crossed round turn*, (opposite page, bottom) made by crossing the second part of the round turn over the first.

If you bend the standing part into a U-shape, you've made a *bight*

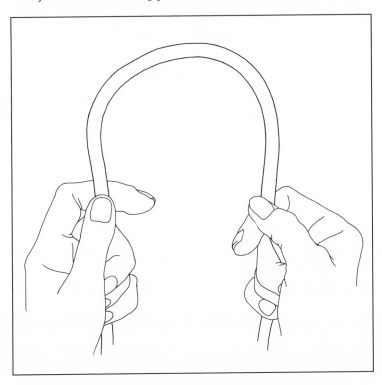

(above). You can weave an end in and around the bight to form knots, or you can tie a knot with the bight, treating it like a sort of double-thickness end, or open the bight up at certain points to fit over other objects, or other parts of the knot. A bight is a very versatile part.

Lay one side of the bight over the other and you get a *loop* (below). This is a clockwise loop, with the end on top of the standing part.

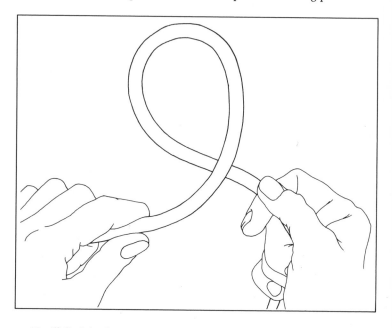

You'll find further jargon, advice, and information as you go along, but at this point, you already know more about the underlying principles of rope and rope work than most people. What follows is largely a matter of detail, to put what you know to work. Time to start tying.

CHAPTER TWO

BINDING KNOTS

B inding knots hold things together. Sails, logs, wiring, rope—all can be held secure with an appropriate binding knot. *Appropriate* means that the line you use is strong enough to hold the load, that it is arranged tightly and intelligently enough to keep the load from moving, and that it can be removed if necessary.

Constrictors are by far the most broadly useful binding knots; they are very quickly made and hold with a tenacious grip. They most often see duty as temporary whippings on rope ends, but they can also clamp together woodworking projects; secure antenna wires to supports; hold splints onto a cracked tiller, mast, or boom in an emergency; or perform any of thousands of other jobs. When drawn very tight, Constrictors can only be removed with a knife, and they can crush fragile items. That's where gentler, removable binding knots such as Marling, Bundle-S, and Swedish Furling come in.

Single Constrictor

TIED WITH THE END

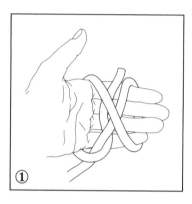 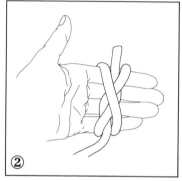

① Start with a crossed round turn (page 15). Bring the end towards you, on the side of the standing part it crossed to. Pass the end over the standing part, then tuck up, under both the standing part and the crossing part.

② The finished knot. Note that structurally it is an overhand knot locked in place by the turn on top of it.

Single Constrictor
TIED IN THE BIGHT

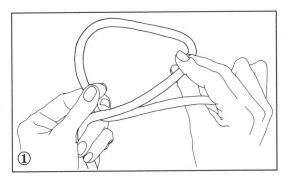

① Start with the loop shown in the introduction (page 16), but with a longer end. Grasp the loop exactly as shown: Your right palm is away from you, with your thumb under the standing part as well as the end.

② Simultaneously turn both hands over. This folds half of the loop down to the front, half down to the back.

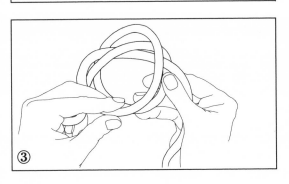

③ The 2 halves of the loop meet below the standing part, forming the knot. When you get the hang of it, this all takes about 3 seconds.

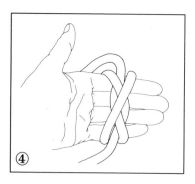

④ The finished knot in place.

Double Constrictor
TIED WITH THE END

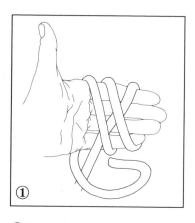

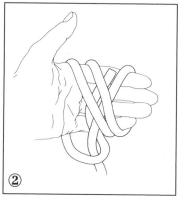

① Start as for a Single Constrictor tied with the end, with a crossed round turn. Follow around again, parallel to the crossing part, to double it. Bring the end towards you on the side of the standing part it crossed to.

② Pass the end over the standing part, then tuck up, under the standing part and both crossing parts.

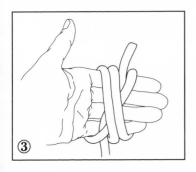

③ The finished knot.

Double Constrictor
TIED IN THE BIGHT

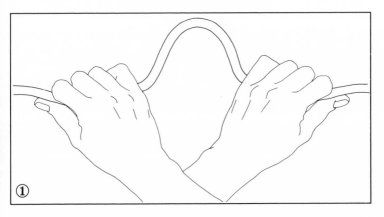

① This knot starts with a Clove Hitch (page 43) tied in the bight by the following "world's fastest method."

Cross your arms, right hand over left and pick up the line, palms down. Leave a bight between your hands.

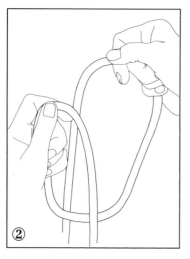

② Uncross your hands, forming 2 loops. The left loop is nearer, the right further away.

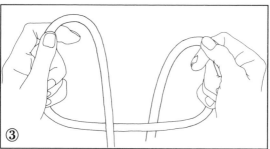

③ Extend your left arm slightly; now the right loop is nearer. Move the left loop behind the right one, forming the Hitch.

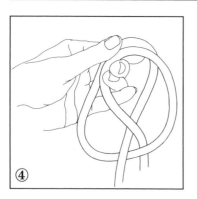

④ A Clove Hitch.

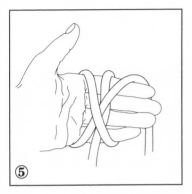

⑤

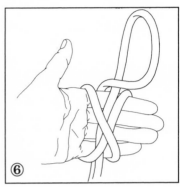

⑥

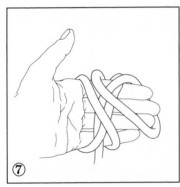

⑦

⑤ To form the Constrictor, place this Clove Hitch on your hand. Pick up the end that is closer to you and lay it over your fingertips, the end going away from you.

⑥ Pull up the middle turn, forming a bight. Twist the front half around, like a door swinging past your fingertips.

⑦ Fold this twisted half down over your fingertips.

⑧ The finished knot.

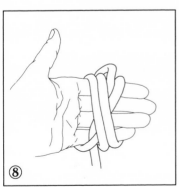

⑧

Marling and Half-Hitching

Marling is a primal operation, a matter of bundling or wrapping things with hitches to hold them in place. The technique goes so far back that we get our terms **marline**, **marlingspike**, and the **marlin** (fish) from it. But Marling is still relevant enough to find uses aboard the most contemporary yachts.

While it can be handy for securing wiring, wrapping packages, and lashing oars and other deck gear in place, Marling is perhaps best known as a technique for attaching the foot of a sail to a boom. It's more precisely adjustable than a spiral lashing, for optional sail shape, and the entire lashing won't come loose if one part is cut.

Note that when the end comes back to its own part after travelling around the boom (or package, oar, etc.), it goes first **over**, then under. If you were to go under first, you'd have a Half-Hitch (fig. 1 page 30), which is less secure. To visualize the difference between the two knots, make them without a hitchee. The Marling Hitch when drawn up forms an Overhand Knot, while the Half-Hitch forms . . . nothing.

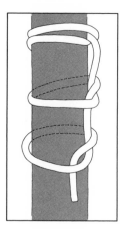

Secure 1 end of the line. Lead the standing part along for a short distance, then pass it completely around the hitchee. Pass the end 1st over, then under, the standing part, forming a knot. Draw up this knot, then lead along a little further and repeat. Finish by securing the end with Half-Hitches or a Seizing (pages 161–163).

Note: If you are lashing a sail to a boom, pass the end 1st through an eyelet, then around the boom, and then form the knot.

Bundle-S

The Marling Hitch is good for containing light, easily handled objects but is no match for a load of heavy cylindrical objects, such as pipe, rod, logs, and so on. These can be awkward to secure and very insistent about getting loose. The neatest, quickest way to deal with them is with a Bundle-S.

Be sure when you start that the S you form is wide enough to project well out from the load. Place "stickers"—spacers that keep the load off the rope—on the ground so you can adjust the hitches.

For light material, finish by securing the two ends together with a Square Knot (page 82). To bind weighty objects securely, put a Bowline (pages 48–61) in one of the ends, reeve the other end through it, haul taut, and finish with two Half-Hitches. This is a form of mechanical advantage called a Trucker's Hitch (page 147).

For extra-long items, make two or more Bundle-S's along the hitchee's length.

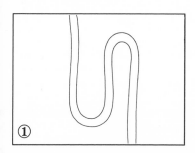

① Lay the line down in an **S**-shape.

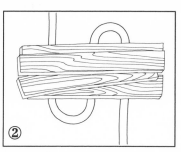

② Lay the objects to be bound across the **S**. Ends and bights project on either side.

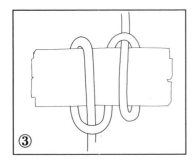 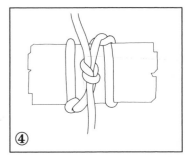

③ Thread each end through the bight directly opposite it.

④ Pull the ends towards each other, tightening the knot around the load. Secure with a Square Knot (page 82). For additional tensioning and security, use a Trucker's Hitch (page 148).

Swedish Furling

A nother bundling hitch, Swedish Furling evolved specifically for securing furled staysails. It goes on quickly, with gratifying neatness, over any size sail. And it comes off zip! zip! zip! like the string on a pet-food bag would if you could ever figure out how to get it started.

If your staysail is equipped with a downhaul (always a good idea), you'll have a perfect furling line already in place, ready to go.

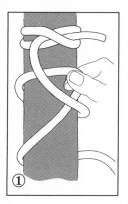

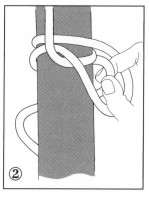

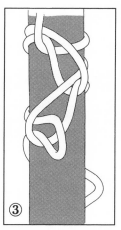

① Practice on a broom handle, pipe, or any other cylindrical object. Secure 1 end of the line at 1 end of the cylinder. Drop a bight over the far side of the cylinder, then bring it around and up, between the cylinder and the standing part. This forms a Half-Hitch on the near side.

② Reach through this bight and pull a 2nd bight up through it from the far side.

③ Repeat this process, pulling bights up from alternate sides. Finish by making 2 Half-Hitches with an extra-long bight. With a sail, these last Hitches can be made around a boom end, or a convenient stanchion, post, etc.

CHAPTER THREE

HITCHES

A Hitch secures one end of a line to an object (which is sometimes the line's own standing part) by wrapping around it and cinching down tight. In this regard, Hitches are like some binding knots, but a Hitch's purpose is not to compress, just to hang on, so that tension can be applied to the line.

With such a simple job to do, you'd think that Hitches would be simple knots. And the good ones are—or at least they are as simple as they can be and still address considerations such as security for slick lines, how great the load is, whether the load is static or cyclic, and what the shape of the hitchee is. Assessing the factors in a given situation will determine which Hitch you tie.

Simple Rolling Hitch

T he Rolling Hitch is a trusty old knot that has adapted itself nicely to contemporary demands. Its twin virtues are that it will hold under lengthwise
pull (most Hitches are designed for right-angle pull) and that its position can
be shifted to adjust tension. The latter virtue was particularly significant in
olden days, since natural-fiber rope shrinks when wet and stretches when dry,
so one needed a simple means of adjusting tension when a belaying pin or cleat
wasn't handy. This knot is still sometimes called the Tent-Line or Taut-Line
Hitch, and since Manila rope is still around, the terms aren't entirely archaic.

Meanwhile, here in the age of synthetic rope, adjustability is still a good
thing. Use the Rolling Hitch to adjust mooring lines in tidal areas, to hang
hammocks, to send tools aloft—learn it, and you'll find countless uses for it.

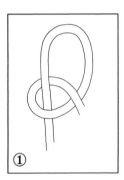 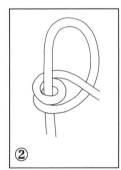 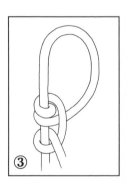

① Make a clockwise loop, end in front of standing part. Pass the end behind the standing part and out through the loop.

② Make a 2nd turn around the standing part, above the 1st turn.

③ Draw up the 1st 2 turns then bring the end down below the loop and make a Half-
Hitch around the standing part. Draw up.

*Note: Always make the turns towards the load. With a loop, the turns always go towards the
end of the loop, since that is where the load will attach. When knotting one line onto another
with a Rolling Hitch, figure out where the load will be coming from, and make the turns in that
direction.*

Camel Hitch

F or slick line, the Camel Hitch is a useful variation. It's just a simple Rolling Hitch with an extra turn and an extra Hitch for a better grip. If even the Camel Hitch won't hold, it's time to make a Deck Stopper (pages 33–34) or Selvagee (pages 35–36) or another Stopper.

In general, think of the Rolling Hitch and Camel Hitch as utility knots for moderate loads. Experiment to get a feel for their range of security, and how that range is affected by relative line size and slickness. Always draw up well before using, choose the Camel Hitch when in doubt, and apply the load slowly, to be sure it will hold.

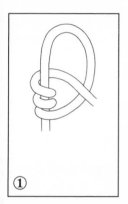 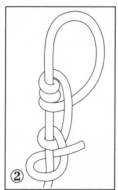 

① Start as for a Rolling Hitch, but pass the end around 3 times instead of 2. Draw up firmly.

② Finish with 2 Half-Hitches instead of 1. Separately draw each Hitch tight.

③ The finished knot.

Note: As with a Rolling Hitch, always make the turns towards the load.

Rigger's Variations on the Rolling and Camel Hitches

When a rigger goes to tie a Rolling or Camel Hitch, it's usually for a heavy-duty job. So riggers came up with industrial-strength versions of the Rolling Hitch and Camel Hitch. They are a bit more trouble to tie, but more resistant to slipping. They are also a bit more resistant to adjusting, so save them for heavy-duty jobs, where adjustability isn't generally an issue.

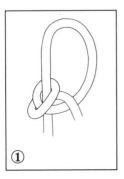

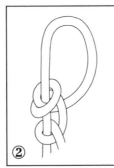

① Start as with the Rolling Hitch, but instead of a round turn, make a crossed round turn. Draw up.

② Finish with a Half-Hitch. This is a more secure, less easily adjustable version of the Rolling Hitch.

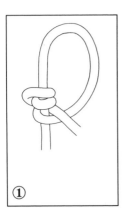

① Make a Camel Hitch, but cross the last turn over the 1st two. Draw up all the turns.

② Finish with 2 Half-Hitches.

New Age Deck Stopper

T he Rolling Hitch and its variations provide ways to keep a line taut under light to medium loads. A Deck Stopper provides a way to keep a line taut under extreme loads.

The Stopper is secured to the deck, next to the standing part of the line being tensioned, usually next to a turning block. With the Stopper wrapped around the standing part, tension on the end can be eased—the Stopper holds the strain while the end is belayed. Once the end is belayed, the Stopper can be removed from the standing part.

So if you've just hoisted the roof beam of a house into place, having a Stopper means that the crew on the fall of the block and tackle doesn't have to stand there trembling with the strain until the roof beam is secured. And if on a sailboat you have two lines to tension but only one winch, a Stopper means you can tension one, then take it off the winch without losing tension, then tension the other.

Stoppers are usually made of lengths of three-strand rope that have been unlaid and braided back together. This makes for a flat surface that grips better than a round rope (more surface area equals more friction). Shown here is a New Age variation made by pulling the core out of a length of double-braid. This should be made from a rope that is at least 50 percent stronger than the rope you'll be stoppering, to compensate for the loss of the core.

Mechanical Stoppers perform much the same function by gripping the rope with cams. But a rope Stopper is good to have around, partly because it's more versatile, since you can move it from place to place, and partly beause it can fill in when one of its mechanical cousins breaks.

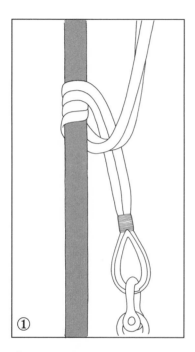

① Pull the core out of a fathom length (6 feet) of double-braid rope. Middle (fold in half) the resulting hollow cover. Seize it around a thimble, and shackle it to the deck.

Pass the 2 tails of the Stopper together, as though starting a Rolling Hitch, making 2 turns towards the thimble.

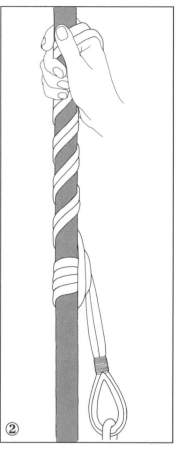

② Make a series of spiral turns away from the thimble, in opposite rotation to the 1st 2 turns. Hold the tails around the standing part with 1 hand. Gradually ease the load onto the Stopper by slacking away on the standing part. When you're sure the Stopper will hold, move the end to a convenient cleat or pin and belay.

Selvagee

A Selvagee is like a Loop Knot Tied in the Bight, in that it enables you to haul heavily on a line at any point along its standing part. Because no Loop Knot is required, you can attach a Selvagee to haul on wire rope. Or you can attach it to rope when a Loop Knot isn't practicable.

For example, if you have a line under tension on a winch, and the turns of the line have become snarled on the drum—this can easily happen if the lead to the winch is wrong or the operator inattentive (see "Winches" pages 150–152)—you will need to put slack into the standing part of the line in order to clear the "wrap" on the winch. As the accompanying illustration shows, one way to deal with this is to apply a Selvagee between the load and the winch, then lead a line from the Selvagee to another winch, or to a block-and-tackle.

A Selvagee can be indispensable for heavy-duty jobs like setting up guy wires and sailboat stays, or for something as simple as hanging a hammock from a shroud.

Selvagees are traditionally made from a thin coil of marline, the circumference of which has been marled to keep the turns from tangling. Under load, this twine doughnut flattens out and grips tenaciously. An effective, modern alternative is to take a long New Age Deck Stopper and secure its ends together with a Strait Bend (pages 77–78). Instant Selvagee.

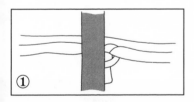

① Remove the core from a fathom (6 feet) of double-braid rope and Strait Bend the ends of the cover together. This makes a Selvagee.

Pass the Selvagee behind the rope or other object you're hitching to, with the bend in the middle and 2 equal length bights on either side.

② Fold the bights across the front, commencing 2 opposite spirals. Note which bight is on top.

35

③ Continue the spirals, crossing the bights in back. The bight that was on top in front is now underneath.

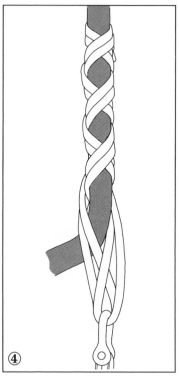

④ Continue the spirals, always alternating which bight in on top. This keeps the 2 bights the same length relative to each other. When you can make no more spirals, shackle or tie the line or block you'll be hauling with through the 2 bights. Take up the load gradually, as with the Deck Stopper, to be sure the Selvagee will hold without slipping.

Note: The Deck Stopper can be passed like a Selvagee, its 2 legs passed independently, and 1 end hitched over the other instead of the ends being held in place by hand.

Round Turn and Two Half-Hitches

T his is the essential Hitch. The round turn distributes the load to lessen chafe where the line bears. It also generates friction, so you can control a load on the line while making the Half-Hitches. This knot is strong, quick, and easy to tie; it will not jam easily, and it's a very easy knot to remember.

That said, bear in mind that it isn't the perfect knot—no knot is. The Round Turn and Two Half-Hitches does have one significant flaw: It lacks security over time. It can slowly untie itself, particularly when made in slick, hard line, and most modern line is both slick and hard.

Therefore, if you plan to leave this Hitch unattended for any length of time, seize the end to the standing part with a Double Constrictor (pages 20–21).

Make a round turn. Make a Half-Hitch and draw it up. Make a 2nd Half-Hitch and draw it up.

Anchor Hitch

*T*his is a more secure variation of the Round Turn and Two Half-Hitches. You simply tuck the end under both parts of the round turn when you make the first Hitch and tie the end to the standing part with a Double Constrictor for ultimate security.

Good, we've gained leave-it-there-and-never-worry-about-it security, but at a price: Because the end must go under both turns, we can no longer make the knot when a load is on the line. The Anchor Hitch is also a little slower to make, and perhaps a little harder to remember.

By now you are probably beginning to see that knots, far from being neutral mechanical fastenings, are highly evolved tools, with distinct strengths and weaknesses. Constrictors, for example, hold extremely well, but are difficult or impossible to undo; Swedish Furling is instantly undone, but only binds lightly; the Rolling Hitch is specialized for lengthwise pull. And so on. This variety is why it is important to develop a vocabulary of knots, so that you can meet any given situation with the appropriate tool. Fortunately, good knots are versatile. So if you only learn good ones, you only have to learn a few.

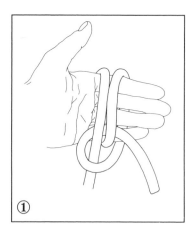

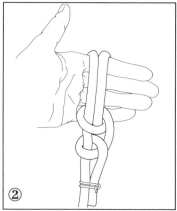

① Make a round turn. Make a Half-Hitch, as with the preceding knot, but this time pass the end under both parts of the turn.

② Draw up. For insurance, add an extra Half-Hitch and a Constrictor (pages 20–21) or Seizing (pages 161–163) to secure the end to the standing part.

Buntline Hitch

T his is the most generally useful Hitch of all, extremely simple and quick to tie, compact, secure, and inclined to jam only under extreme loads. Even then, it can be picked apart with a spike.

The Buntline Hitch is a very old knot, but not widely known today. This is changing, once again in response to the advent of synthetic lines. The Buntline Hitch holds admirably in slick synthetics, better than the Round Turn and Two Half-Hitches, and is much less bother than the Anchor Hitch. It is the preferred knot for anything but extreme loads. Try it as a replacement in many circumstances for the weaker, less secure, more space-consuming Bowline.

When slipped, the Buntline Hitch can be cleared away more cleanly and easily than any other comparably secure Slipped Hitch.

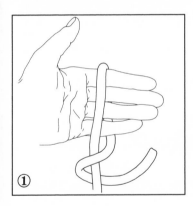

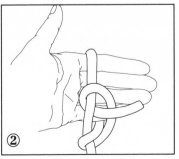

① Make a turn around your hand, then make a turn around the standing part.

② Bring the end up above the turn that is around the standing part, and make a Half-Hitch around the standing part.

③ Draw the turn and Half-Hitch tight, then snug the knot up against the hitchee.

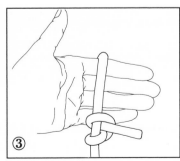

Marlingspike Hitch

A ny knot worth tying is worth drawing up so that it won't come apart or distort. With most knots this requires only light tension, something you can do with your bare hands. But some knots—Constrictors, Lashings, Seizings, etc.—require a good hard pull before they're usable, and a good hard pull will hurt your hands, particularly if the line is small.

That's when you need a Marlingspike Hitch. It's a handle you can temporarily install on a line for painless tensioning, and then instantly remove.

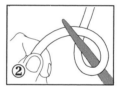
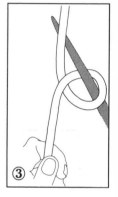

① Secure one end of the line. Hold the standing part in one hand, spike in the other. Lay the spike on the line, forming an **X**.

② Make a turn around the spike. Point the spike towards the secured end, so the turn becomes a loop around the spike tip.

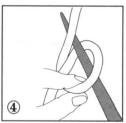

③ Put the tip of the spike behind the standing part.

④ Grasp the loop that is around the spike, pull a little slack into it, and fold it towards the tip.

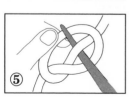

⑤ Drop the loop over the tip to form the Hitch.

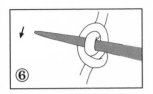

⑥ The finished knot. Pull only in the direction indicated or the knot will jam.

Carabiner Hitch

A carabiner is a type of shackle developed by mountaineers for their climbing lines. It has found its way aboard sailboats, primarily as a safety-line shackle, since its wide-opening, spring-loaded jaws provide a quick, secure attachment, even to bulky items such as stanchions.

The carabiner can also be used as a brake, for controlled descent from aloft. That's where the Carabiner Hitch comes in: With it one can hang securely in place, or feed slack through to come down. Even if you have someone on deck lowering you under complete control, it is excellent practice to hitch a separate insurance line to your bosun's chair or safety harness, in case the primary halyard should fail.

To prevent accidental opening, use spring- or screw-lock carabiners. If these are not available, be certain, as shown here, that you start the knot by passing a bight on the side of the standing part that is away from the carabiner jaw.

① Clip the carabiner onto the line.

② Grasp the standing part below the carabiner. Bring the line up, over its own part, then down behind the carabiner. Open the trigger and pull the standing part into the carabiner.

With sufficiently large, stiff rope, this hitch generates enough friction to hold your weight. You can lower yourself by feeding slack up through the Hitch.

③ If a single Hitch slips under your weight, bring the standing part up once more. This time pass it *behind* its own part and bring it down in *front* of the carabiner. Finish, as before, by pulling the standing part into the carabiner.

④ The finished Hitch, doubled. To untie, reverse the above steps.

BOSUN'S-CHAIR APPLICATION

The carabiner is attached to the chair or to a safety harness. Two lines come to the chair: One is controlled by a crew member on deck; the other is a belayed safety line, and the carabiner is hitched to its standing part.

Clove Hitch
TIED WITH THE END

T he Clove Hitch is a very simple, very well known, but not very secure
knot. Confine its use to light-duty, short-term applications, such as teth-
ering a dog or roping off an area. And even then, don't use this knot on
square-sectioned objects; it's prone to "walk" right off. For most jobs, the
Buntline Hitch is preferable.

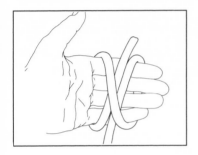

Make a crossed round turn. Bring the end
towards you, on the side of the standing
part it crossed to. Pass the end up, under
the crossing part. Draw up.

Clove Hitch
TIED IN THE BIGHT

S ometimes you simply need a Hitch in a hurry. You don't have time to be
picky about ultimate security or strength, or ease of untying—you've just
got to get a line on something right now. In such a situation, the lowly Clove
Hitch Tied in the Bight can be a godsend, especially when made by this
"world's fastest method."

   And when you get a moment, you can render any Clove Hitch more secure
by adding an extra Hitch to it. This can be done either in the bight or by passing the end.

To make this knot, see the beginning of the Double Constrictor Tied in the Bight (pages 21–23).

43

Knute Hitch

Many tools commonly used aboard sailboats (sheath knives, mar-lingspikes, electric drills, etc.) have small holes in their handles for attaching lanyards. When working aloft, or even when on deck in a seaway, it's good sense to have all your tools on lanyards. The Knute Hitch is the most secure, compact, easily removed "small hole" Hitch.

Note: For this Hitch to work, it is important that the lanyard stock be just small enough to fit, doubled through the lanyard hole. A Buntline Hitch is ideal for lanyarding tools with larger holes; a Double Constrictor is a good method for attaching lanyards to holeless tools.

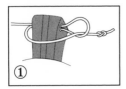  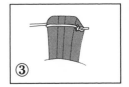

① Tie a Figure-Eight Knot (page 176) in the end of a piece of twine. Slip a bight of the twine through the tool's lanyard hole. It should just fit. Pass the end through the bight.

② Adjust so that the end is just beyond the bight and the twine is fairly snug around the tool. Pull on the standing part. This will cause the bight to be drawn into the hole. The Figure-Eight Knot will fetch up against the hole.

③ The finished knot. To undo, pull on the Figure-Eight Knot.

Ring Hitch

When *you think of the Ring Hitch, think of sail ties and shackles: sail ties, because when the sail is up the Ring Hitch is the tidiest way to secure them to handrails, stanchions, etc.; shackles, because a strip of leather secured with a Ring Hitch to the eye of a snap-shackle piston makes a perfect little lanyard for easy opening.*

The Ring Hitch has many other uses, for everything from saddle girths to baggage tags. Whatever you use it for, just be sure that the load comes on both ends. Otherwise, it may slip.

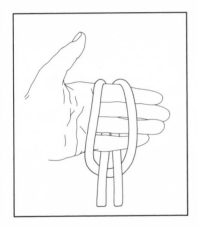

Drop a bight over the hitchee. Pass both ends through the bight, below the hitchee. Pull tight.

CHAPTER FOUR

LOOP KNOTS

L ines can only go to work when you attach them to something. Most often, the handiest method of attachment is a Loop Knot. While Hitches are generally more compact and secure, Loop Knots are just plain expedient. For one thing, they don't rely on the presence of a separate object to give them form—if you slide a Hitch off its hitchee, for example, it becomes a snarl or dissolves altogether. But a Loop Knot is an independent structure, so you don't always have to tie and untie it for each job. For another thing, Loop Knots can be simpler to untie, because the end is not jammed up against something. Finally, you can make a Loop Knot anywhere along the length of a line, without using the end.

Loop Knots can't do everything. They can't, for instance, grab securely onto something, the way a Hitch can. But for a quick tie-up to posts, rings, rails, etc., they're perfect.

Fingertip Bowline

One often needs to make a Bowline in midair, to have it ready to drop over a piling, bollard, winch, or such. In this case, the Fingertip Bowline is the way to go.

Note that with this technique the loop of the knot faces you, while with the Spilled-Hitch Bowline (page 51) it faces away from you. Learn both techniques and you'll avoid the acrobatics people sometimes go through because they only learned to tie the knot with the loop one way, and circumstances present them with the necessity of having it the other way.

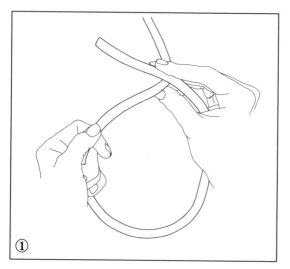

① Form a counterclockwise loop, end on top, and grasp the standing part with your right hand, which also holds the end. This is similar to the beginning of the Marlingspike Hitch (pages 40–41), and subsequent moves here will parallel the forming of that knot.

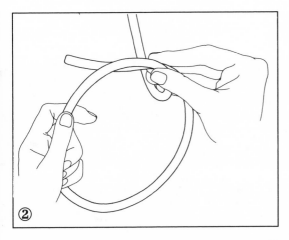

② Make a turn around the end by dropping the end down behind the loop . . .

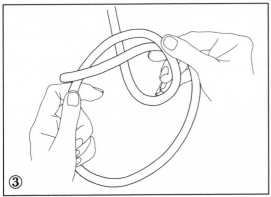

③ . . . then bringing it up inside the loop as shown. This forms a 2nd loop.

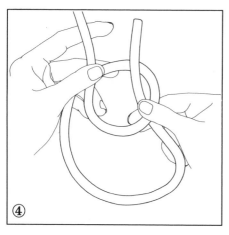

④

④ Continue bringing the end up until it is parallel with the stand-ing part. Hold the stand-ing part up with your left index finger, and pass the end behind it.

⑤ Grasp the end with your left hand and drop it back into the loop that is around your fingers.

⑥ To draw up, hold the standing part in one hand, the end and side of this loop in the other hand. Pull.

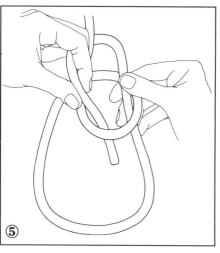

⑤

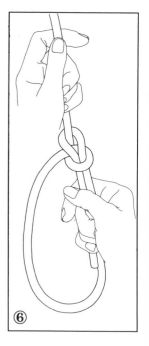

⑥

Spilled-Hitch Bowline

To attach a line to an object like a rail or sail clew, use the Spilled-Hitch method. Because it starts with the supremely simple Half-Hitch, this method is mindlessly easy to start. And because the Hitch, once spilled, automatically orients the end for the final tuck, it is gratifyingly easy to finish.

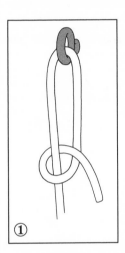
①

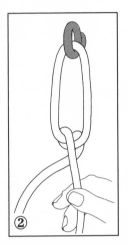
②

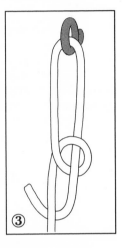
③

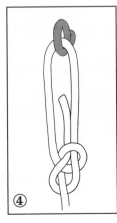
④

① Thread the end through the object you're tying to. Make a Half-Hitch by passing the end over the standing part, then back under the standing part and over the end's own part.

② By pulling the end towards you, you will "spill" the Half-Hitch into the standing part.

③ Pass the end behind the standing part, away from the Spilled-Hitch.

④ Pass the end into the loop and draw up, as for the Fingertip Bowline.

Round Turn Spilled-Hitch Bowline
LOCKED

For centuries, sailors have counted on the Bowline's ability to stay put under any circumstance. But modern synthetic lines are often much slicker than the natural-fiber lines of the past, and modern Bowlines sometimes slip.

So any time you want some cheap security insurance, "lock" your Bowlines. This is particularly recommended for situations in which the load comes and goes, as with dinghy painters, sheets, and slings, when you can't count on a steady strain to help hold things together.

The Locked Bowline takes a little longer to tie, but then you don't have to worry about retying. And you can untie it as easily as a regular Bowline, even after a heavy load.

If there's any danger of chafe on the eye of a Bowline—say you're making a line off to a small-diameter ring—then beginning with a round turn will help distribute the load over more fibers, thus reducing chafe.

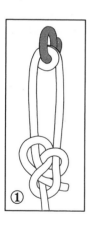

① For better distribution of strain, make a round turn through the object you're tying to. Form a loose Spilled-Hitch Bowline.

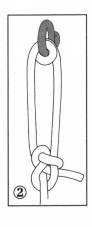

② Bring the end around and pass it under the 2 parallel parts at the "neck" of the knot. Draw up. (The same knot can be used for the Fingertip Bowline.)

Running Bowline

To make a grip-tight sling, or to get an eye around an unusually large object, or to send a halyard down from aloft "on its own part" (so the end doesn't flail out of reach in the breeze), make a Running Bowline.

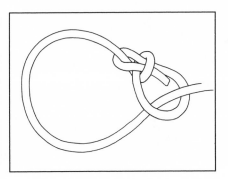

Tie a Fingertip Bowline, with the end *around* the standing part.

Slipknot Bowline

The Slipknot Bowline is a downright fun, flashy knot that also happens to be very useful in a pinch. You can have the Slipknot ready in one hand, while the other hand passes the end through whatever you're tying to. Then, instead of stopping to tie, you form a Bowline, instantly, with a tug on the standing part.

So if you're drifting past a piling, or trying to get an unsecured clew under control or need to work in a cramped, uncomfortable place such as under a car, first make a Slipknot, then materialize a Bowline.

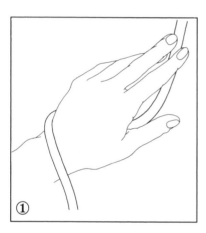

① Pass the end around or through the object you're tying to. The standing part is toward you. Bring your hand across your body and behind the standing part. Raise your hand up towards you, then out to the side.

②, ③ Turn your hand palm-away from you and drop it down outside the standing part. Continue turning your hand so that you form a loop around your hand with the standing part in the space between your thumb and forefinger. Raise your hand and. . .

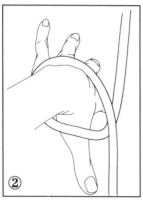

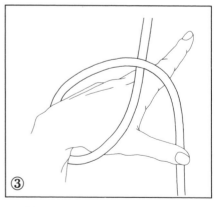

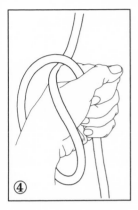

④ . . . grasp the standing part and pull the standing part out through the loop. This forms a Slipknot.

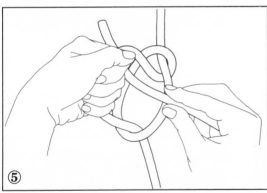

⑤ With your free hand, pick up the end and pass it through the eye of the Slipknot. Leave a long end hanging out.

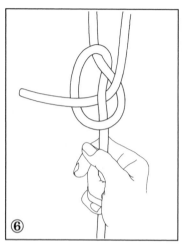

⑥ Let go of the end and pull on the standing part.

⑦ This capsizes the Slipknot, forming a Bowline.

⑧ The finished knot.

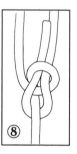

Hawser Bowline

LEVER

W ith a big rope—an inch in diameter or larger—the sheer mass and stiffness of the material can defeat your attempts to form a Bowline by the Spilled, Fingertip, or Slipknot methods. To replace the Spilled-Hitch method, you use your arm as a lever and your wrist as a fulcrum to get the starting loop into position. It's a judolike move, and very effective. After that, it's just a matter of passing the end along its usual route.

Warning: Be certain that there's no chance of a load coming on the line while you are tying the knot.

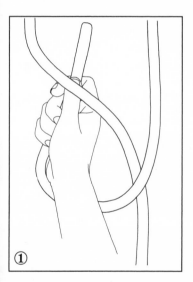

① Pass the end around the object you're securing it to. Hold the end so that it comes out between your thumb and index finger. Pass the end over the standing part, forming a loop. Bring the end and your hand up inside the loop.

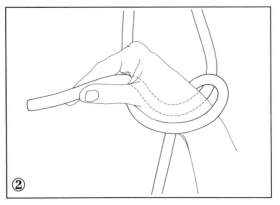

② Bring your hand back towards you. This will "lever" the loop into the standing part. The loop will encircle your wrist.

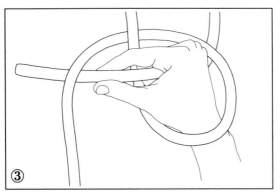

③ Pass the end behind the standing part, away from the loop.

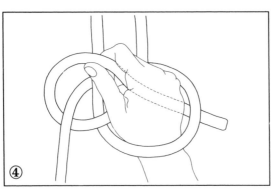

④ Let go of the end, then reach over the standing part to grab it again. Use your other hand to assist here.

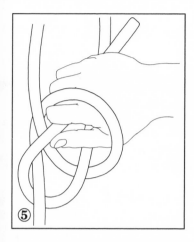

⑤ Pull your hand out of the loop, taking the end with it. This forms the Bowline.

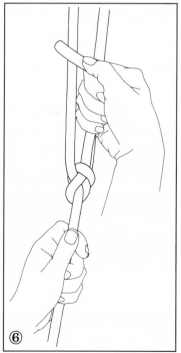

⑥ Draw up by pulling on the end and standing part.

Hawser Bowline

ON DECK

T he On-Deck Bowline is for truly huge rope, the kind you can't even pick up readily. This Bowline can be formed by shifting short lengths of the line around, which saves your back.

The On-Deck Bowline is an industrial-strength version of the Slipknot Bowline; it capsizes into being when the load comes on.

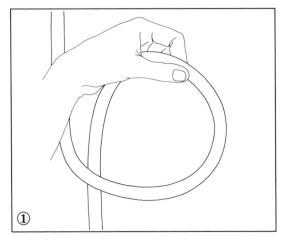

① Make a counterclockwise loop flat on the deck (or ground or floor), with the end under the standing part. Grasp the top of the loop.

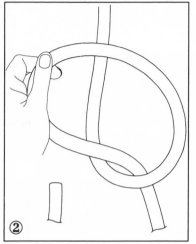

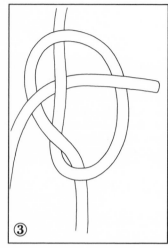

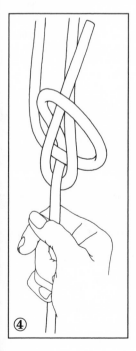

② Pull the top of the loop over so that it rests on the standing part. Bring the end up on the left side of the standing part.

③ Pass the end from left to right: over the loop, under the standing part, and over the other side of the loop.

④ A pull on the standing part will capsize the arrangement into a Bowline.

Good Luck Knot

The Good Luck Knot is a decorative loop, which is to say that it's tricky to tie and is inclined to jam. But it makes up for these flaws with a particularly pleasing appearance—and spiritual significance.

In ancient China, where this knot originated, a square was the symbol of Earth—the great, solid reality. And the cross signified the abstract, the spiritual. It was in the harmonious mingling of these opposites, as symbolized in the faces of this knot, that good luck was said to arise.

Use the Good Luck Knot for lanyards, leashes, or other permanent loops. Or do as the sailors of Nelson's navy did and tie kerchieves and scarves with it. The Tars called this knot the True Square Knot. But you can tie it for luck.

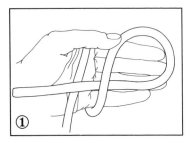

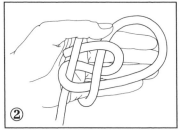

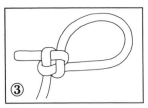

① Make a round turn around your hand, then fold the end down to form a clockwise loop on your palm. The end is under the turn on the right, over the turn on the left.

② Thread the end under both turns left to right, then over 1, under 1, right to left.

③ Draw up carefully to form the finished knot. To avoid capsizing, keep the face of the knot square as you make it smaller and tighter.

Note: The Good Luck Knot may be tied as a Bend. Make a round turn with one end, then thread the other end in from the right, under and over, back to the right, under both, and back to the left, over and under.

Single Lineman's Loop

J ust as there are hitches that can be made "in the bight" (Belay to Winch, Carabiner Hitch, Swedish Furling, Constrictors, etc.), so there are Loop Knots that can be formed without using the end. This means that you don't have to drag the end all the way through everything when you want to make an eye—say, for hanging a block—in the middle of a great long piece of rope.

The Single Lineman's Loop is the premier knot in this class. Structurally analogous to the Strait Bend (pages 77–78), it is strong, stable, and easily tied and untied. Unlike many other Loop Knots, it will not distort if the load only comes on one end. And since it leads at a perfect right angle to the standing part, the load can equitably come on the loop from any direction.

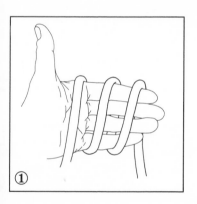

① Make 3 turns on your hand.

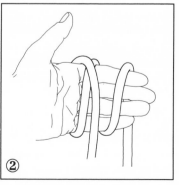

② Move the innermost (closest to your thumb) turn over to the middle.

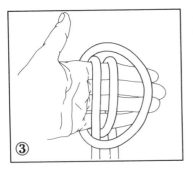

③ Pull slack into the new innermost turn. Pass it over both the other turns, towards your fingertips.

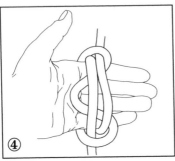

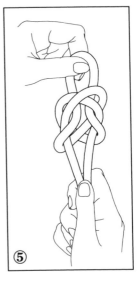

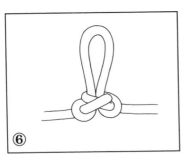

④ Now pass it under both turns, back towards your thumb.

⑤ Remove the knot from your hand. Draw up firmly.

⑥ The finished knot.

Double Lineman's Loop

T his is a case of "learn one knot, get one free." By making a loose Single Lineman's Loop, then taking one extra step, you end up with a handsome, secure Double Loop Knot. It's just the thing for an emergency bosun's chair, or a sling for a ladder, or a low-chafe shackle attachment, or a Trucker's Hitch (page 148) loop.

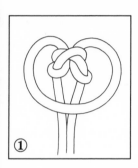

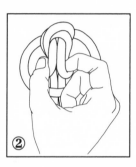

① Start with a loosely made Single Lineman's Loop. Hold the knot and standing parts with one hand. With your other hand, open up the loop and fold it down over the knot.

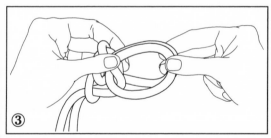

② Pull up on the 2 bights that lead directly to the loop.

③ Draw the 2 bights up to form 2 loops. The original loop will draw up around the 2 standing parts. If the bights do no draw out readily, try holding the knot itself with one hand while pulling up on the bights with the other.

④ The finished knot.

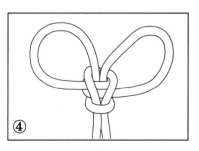

Bowline on the Bight

By no means the equal of the Double Lineman's Loop in terms of lead or security, the Bowline on the Bight is worth knowing, since it is easier to form large loops with it, especially in ponderously large line. Like the Carrick Bend (pages 79–80) and the Hawser Bowline on the Deck (pages 60–61), it can be made on deck, so you only have to deal with short sections of heavy line at a time.

Unlike the Double Lineman's Loop, the Bowline on the Bight is not secure unless both standing parts share the strain evenly. If there isn't enough line to belay both, make a Bowline on the Bight with a Bowline on it.

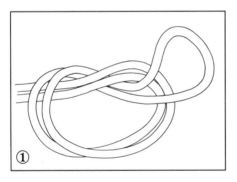

① Form a bight. Form an Overhand Knot by passing the bight behind the standing part, then out through the loop.

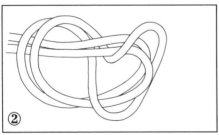

② Open the bight up and fold it around behind the Overhand Knot.

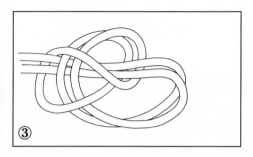

③ Pass the bight clear around, until it reaches the standing part.

④ Take hold of the 2 uppermost parts of the Overhand Knot. Pull on the sides that lead to the bight to form the knot.

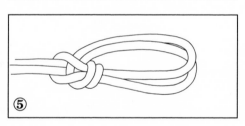

⑤ The finished knot.

Angler's Loop

FOR BUNGY CORD

T his good old knot was originally used to form an eye in fishing line. Modern synthetic fiber—too slick for the knot to hold—made it obsolete, but the Angler's Loop has new life in another modern material: bungy cord. It seems that Bowlines and other Loop Knots crawl out of bungy under load or come undone when the load is off. But the Angler's Loop just hangs in there. A case of an old knot finding a new home.

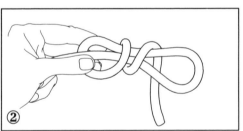

① Make a long, counterclockwise loop, end behind standing part.

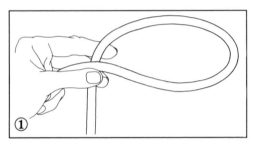

② Bring the end up towards you and make a round turn around the loop.

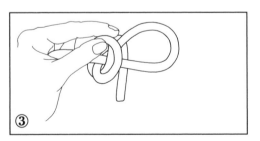

③ Pass the 1st part of the round turn over the 2nd part and down through the eye of the loop.

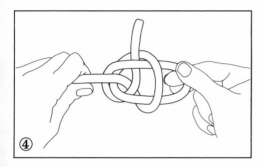

④ To draw up, pull on the eye and the standing part, then on the end.

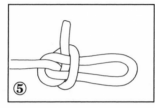

⑤ The finished knot.

CHAPTER FIVE

BENDS

A Bend is a knot that joins two lines together. Of all the possible interweavings that do this, only a few are generally used, because only a few have all of the following virtues: strength, security (won't slip), stability (won't capsize), ease of tying, and ease of untying (won't jam under heavy loads).

Even among Bends which share these virtues, circumstances may favor one over the others. For instance, the Double Sheet Bend (pages 74–75), is especially suited to lines of different diameter or consistency, and the Carrick Bend (pages 79–80) to lines of extraordinary size. So before you join two lines, think about the nature of those lines and what you expect them to do. Then tie accordingly.

Study this section extra carefully and work up a versatile Bend vocabulary. It might be a while before you have to extend a towing line or temporarily add to a cut halyard, but when the time comes, you'll know how to do the job well.

Single Sheet Bend

T his is the basic utility bend. It holds well in Manila and hemp, but can
slip in synthetics, particularly braided constructions.

*The technique shown here is one evolved by weavers to repair broken
threads in their looms. It is the fastest way to tie the Single Sheet Bend, and
it's also a way that guarantees the ends will finish on the same side of the
standing part. Tied by other methods, there's a fifty-fifty chance that the ends
will be diagonally opposed, resulting in a less secure knot.*

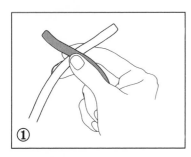

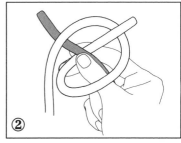

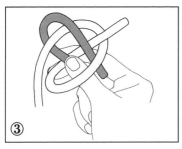

① Cross the right end over the left. Hold
the ends, at the cross, in your right hand.

② Pick up the standing part on the left.
Make a counterclockwise turn with it
behind its own end, then lay it down
between the 2 ends.

③ Take the end on your left and drop it
over the standing part you just laid down
between the 2 ends. Then drop the end
into the loop, next to your right thumb.

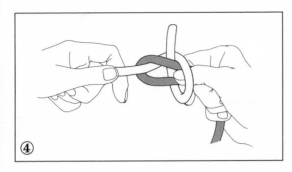

④ To draw up, hold the end and standing part in your right hand and pull on the other standing part with your left hand.

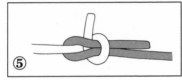

⑤ The finished knot.

Double Sheet Bend

For joining together stiff, slick synthetic line, or just to be extra safe, use the Double Sheet Bend. It is much more slip-resistant than the Single, and almost as quick to tie. Just be sure that the second turn goes **below** the first. Unlike the Single, this knot cannot be drawn up properly just by pulling on the ends; take time to work the slack out before putting this or any other Bend to use.

The Double Sheet Bend is the only Bend to use when joining lines of dissimilar size, or when one line is considerably stiffer or slicker than the other. The smaller, more supple, and/or slicker line makes the turns. The larger, stiffer, and/or less slick line only needs to make a U-turn to finish the knot.

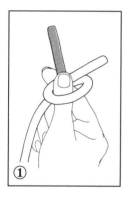 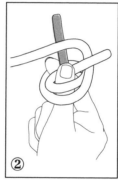 

① Start as for the Single Sheet Bend, but make the turn around *both* ends.

② Make a 2nd turn, *below* the 1st. Then bring the standing part down between the 2 ends, as for the Single Sheet Bend.

③ Drop the left-hand end down through the loops, alongside its own standing part, to finish.

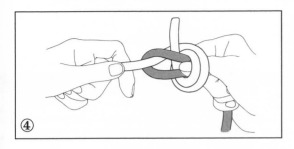

④ Start drawing up as for the Single Sheet Bend, but pause to pull up on the upper end for a firm knot.

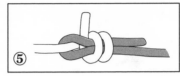

⑤ The finished knot.

Single Becket Bend

*W*hen joining an end to an Eye Splice or Loop Knot you only have one end to work with, and so cannot use the weaver's method for tying the Sheet Bend. Instead, thread the end through as shown.

Because the technique and configuration are different, this is called a Becket (eye) Bend, to distinguish it from the structurally identical Sheet Bend.

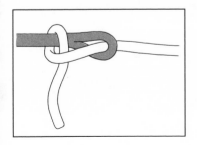

Pass the end up towards you, through the eye. Pass the end down, then up behind the eye, then down between the eye and its own part. Draw up.

Double Becket Bend

J *ust as with the Double Sheet Bend, slick or unequal size line calls for the more secure Double Becket Bend.*

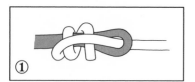

① Tie a Single Becket Bend loosely. Pass the end around the eye and under its own part once more. Draw up.

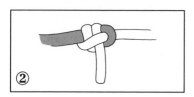

② The finished Double Becket Bend.

Strait Bend

U *seful though the Sheet Bends are, they do have their limitations: They can jam tight under extreme loads; one end sticks out at a shallow angle, ready to snag on whatever it passes; and even the Double can slip when the load is intermittent. So for ultimate security, perfect right-angle lead of the ends, and ease of untying—as well as superior strength—use the Strait Bend.*

The Strait Bend is structurally analogous to the Lineman's Loop (pages 63–64).

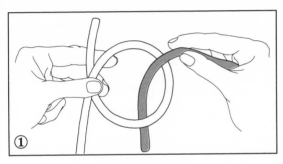

① Make a clockwise loop, end behind the standing part. Hold in your left hand. Drop the other end into this loop.

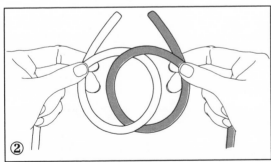

② Make a counterclockwise loop with the 2nd end, also end behind the standing part. The 2 interlinked loops form an elliptical eye between them.

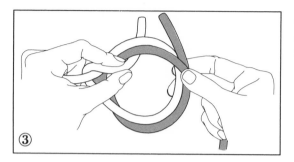

③, ④ Pass both ends into this eye, away from you.

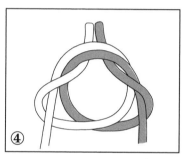

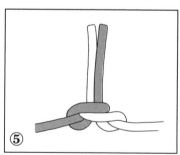

⑤ Draw up by holding the knot with 1 hand and pulling in succession on each end and each standing part.

Carrick Bend
SEIZED

T his ancient bend is suited to large-diameter rope. It has no sharp turns (big rope is hard to turn and once drawn up, hard to straighten) and it can be made with the two lines on the deck; you only have to shift small sections at a time. The Carrick Bend is also easy to remember: Once you get it set up, you simply pass the end in a regular over-and-under sequence.

The seizings keep the knot from collapsing into its drawn-up form (see below), but they do not bear much of a load. A series of Double Constrictors, drawn very tight, is an expedient way to seize.

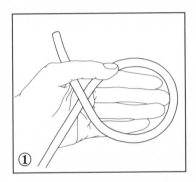

① Form a clockwise loop, end on top of the standing part. Hold this loop on your left palm.

②, ③ Lay the other end towards you, on top of the loop. Begin passing this end clockwise in a regular under-and-over sequence: under the standing part, over the end, under one side of the loop, over its own standing part, and under the other side of the loop.

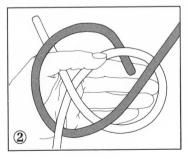

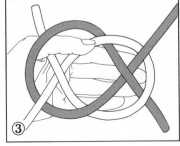

④ For an extremely easy-to-untie bend, seize the ends to the standing parts, either with several Double Constrictors each (pages 20–21) or with Two-Leg Seizings (pages 161–63).

Carrick Bend

DRAWN UP

I f you tie a loose Carrick Bend with sufficiently long ends and do not seize it, it will draw up under load into the form shown here. Less trouble to make, more trouble to untie.

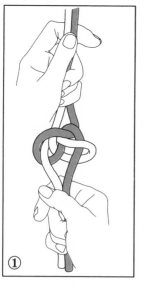

① Grasp both ends and both standing parts. Pull.

② The finished knot.

Toggled Bend

T he ultimate in ease of untying, the Toggled Bend incorporates an instantly removable toggle (pin) in its structure. Yank out the pin and the knot disappears.

Why would one want a disappearing knot? To cast off a towline, remove and hang up a hammock or awning (one line with an eye in it remains attached to the rigging), or to set moorings (a little strop suspends the mooring beneath the boat; a pull on the toggle releases the mooring). Toggles are also practical alternatives to shackles on traditionally rigged vessels, for attaching preventer tackle, running-back tackle, sheet-lead blocks, and other often shifted gear. And a toggled dock-line makes a nifty getaway setup when you're leaving a dock shorthanded.

Be certain that your toggle is equal to the load it's expected to bear, and that it has a lanyard attached to it, both for ease of removal and to keep it from dropping into the drink once removed.

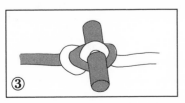

① Start with 2 loops, preferably Eye Splices. (If you use a Loop Knot, there is a danger that the knots will hang up when the toggle is released.) Thread 1 eye through the other.

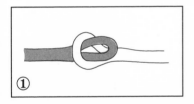

② One eye is empty; pull a bight of the other eye's standing part up through it and insert the toggle in this bight. Draw up.

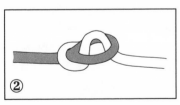

③ The finished knot.

Simple Square Knot

The Square Knot is one knot that everyone knows—you tie your shoes with a form of it. So it's not surprising that people resort to it to tie lines together. Unfortunately, the Square Knot is inclined to capsize (distort under load into another form) and come undone. All it takes is a snag on one end, an unexpected jerk, or even one line's being wetter, stiffer, or larger than the other. It is the last knot you want to use as primary load-bearer.

On the other hand, it is the preferred knot for finishing off lashings, since the turns of the lashing take most of the strain and preclude any jolts to the knot.

① Lay 1 end on top of the other.

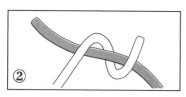

② Wrap whichever end is on top around the other end.

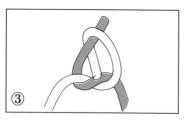

③ Recross the ends. The end that was on top at the beginning is on top again. Wrap it once more around the other end. Pull both ends to draw up.

④ The finished knot.

Slipped Square Knot

When securing a furled or reefed sail, the load is low and the consequences of a knot's failing are not likely to be serious. What you want is a knot that is quick to make and adequately secure. The knot of choice is the Slipped Square Knot. (This is why the Square Knot is sometimes called a Reef Knot.)

The knot is "slipped" for easy removal. Usually only one side is slipped, as it is easier to tie this way and is secure enough for the job.

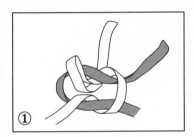

① Begin as for a Simple Square Knot (page 82). Form the 2nd Overhand Knot, but only pull a *bight* through. Draw up by pulling on this bight and the other end.

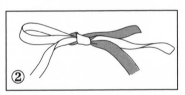

② The finished knot. Release by pulling on the bight's end.

CHAPTER SIX

SPLICES

EYE SPLICES

An Eye Splice is a permanent Loop in the end of a line. It is slow to tie and impractical to untie between uses, so it lacks the versatility of the Bowline or Hitch. But every knot weakens the line it is tied in—Bowlines by about 45 percent, most Hitches by about 35 percent. The Eye Splice, made in three-strand or double-braid rope, shares the load so evenly among the component strands that when properly made it will weaken a line by 5 percent or less. It is the only Loop to use when loads are extreme.

It is also the most compact of all Loops, so it is useful even in low-load situations, if chafe or tight spaces are a consideration.

Three-Strand Eye Splice

T hink of this as weaving. The three working ends cross the three standing-part strands and interweave, like a weft and warp. Because rope is round, the very beginning is a little complicated—you have to introduce the ends in such a way that they all bear an even strain right from the start.

There are a number of possible entries. The one shown here is extremely fair and is well suited to slick synthetics since the doubled first tuck of strand number one holds things together nicely while you tuck numbers two and three. This entry also makes for a snugger-than-usual fit around a thimble—a metal or plastic collar that lines the inside of the eye of the splice. Without the thimble, the rope would chafe as it made a tight turn around a shackle. A thimble is not necessary when the eye goes over large smooth objects like posts and bollards, since the strain is distributed over a greater area.

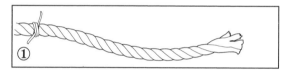

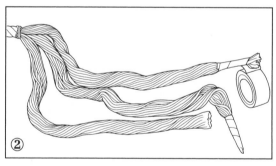

① With a piece of waxed sail twine, apply a Double Constrictor (pages 20–21) 6–7 inches from the end of a piece of 1/2-inch-diameter, 3-strand Dacron line. (The distance of the Constrictor from the end will vary with line diameter and the number of tucks desired. With larger line, each strand will have to travel further to complete a given number of tucks. Slick line, such as nylon, will require more tucks—5 or 6—than coarser line, such as spun Dacron or Manila, which will require 3 or 4.)

② Unlay the strands up to the Constrictor. "Milk" the ends one at a time by grasping firmly by the constrictor, then sliding your hand towards the end. This will make the strands flat and ribbonlike, for a fairer splice. Tape the ends after milking.

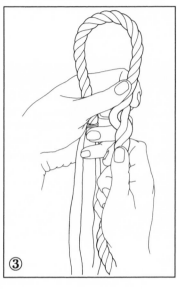

③ Form a bight the size of the desired eye. The bight is up, the end on the left. Grasp the standing part opposite the Constrictor with both hands, as shown. Move your hands towards each other while twisting the standing part to open the lay, raising the strands into low bights. Hold the leftmost (innermost) bight open and let go of the standing part with your right hand.

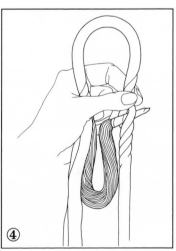

④ Tuck the rightmost (innermost) end-strand through the open bight, from left to right. This is end-strand #1.

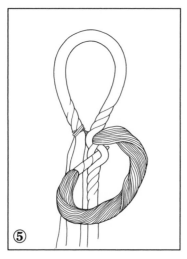

⑤ Immediately tuck strand #1 once more, over 1 standing part strand and under the next, repeating the twist-to-open procedure to raise the bight to tuck under. End-strand #1 now goes under, over, and under, from left to right.

⑥ Pick up the middle end-strand. This is strand #2. Tuck it under the standing-part strand that #1 went over. Tuck it once only, with #1 between it and the eye.

⑦ Turn the eye over. The last untucked end-strand, #3, is on your right. In the middle, at the base of the eye, there is a standing-part strand with nothing tucked under it.

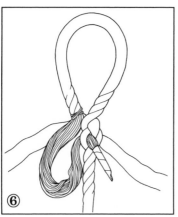

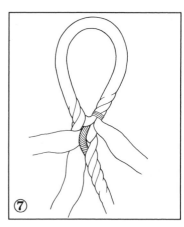

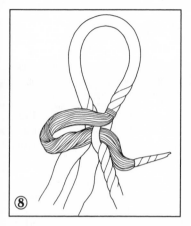

⑧

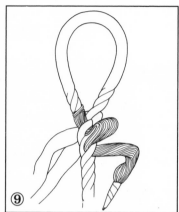

⑨

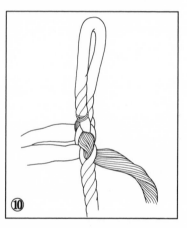

⑩

⑧ Tuck end-strand #3 under this central standing-part strand, from *left to right* once. This completes the first and trickiest row of tucks.

⑨ All strands now exit at the same level, or "a-tier." Fair them by pulling on each 1 in turn, to snug the Constrictor in close. Then take any end-strand (we show #3) and tuck it over 1 and under 1 from left to right.

⑩ Take a 2nd end-strand and tuck it over 1 and under 1 from left to right. (You have turned the eye to expose a new strand.)

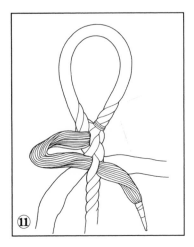

⑪ Finish the 2nd row of tucks by tucking the remaining strand over and under. Note that it passes *between* the 2 previously tucked strands. Fair again after each row of tucks.

⑫ Repeat for at least 2 more rows of tucks for spun Dacron, at least 3 more for filament Dacron and nylon. Roll the finished splice firmly between your hands or underfoot for a final fairing. Whip ("Three-Strand Whipping," pages 159–160) or tie a Double Constrictor (pages 20–21) over the last tuck before trimming the ends. Or leave the tuck unwhipped and cut the ends a full rope-diameter in length.

SHACKLE SPLICE
CROWN SPLICE

T he Shackle Splice is a thimbleless alternative to the Eye Splice. Because
each strand crosses the shackle independently, there is three times the
area of rope bearing on the shackle. The result is a more even distribution of
strain, and minimized chafe.

On a halyard, the shorter overall length of the Shackle Splice means you get
a couple of inches more hoist before the splice hits the sheave. And on pendants
that shackle to mooring-buoy chains, the Shackle Splice eliminates the problem
of chafe caused by the thimble's shifting about in the stretchy nylon rope eye.

Made without a shackle, this knot becomes a Back Splice, a sort of built-
in handle at the end of water-bucket lanyards, leashes, and the like.

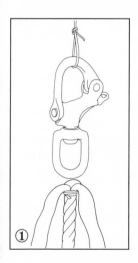

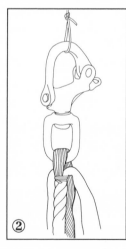

① Apply a Constrictor (pages 20–21) a short distance from the rope end, say 8-10 inches, for a typical halyard of 1/2 inch diameter. Unlay the strands to the Constrictor and, holding the rope upright, arrange them petallike, as shown. Suspend the shackle above the rope, or have an assistant hold it there.

② Pick up the strand nearest you (#1), and pass it *away* from you, through the shackle. Lay the end down between the other 2 ends.

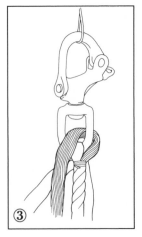

③ Pick up the strand on your right (#2) and pass it *towards* you, through the eye of the shackle, and lay it down between the other 2 strands, to the left of the bight of #1.

④ Pick up the strand on your left (#3). Pass it over #2 and under the bight of #1.

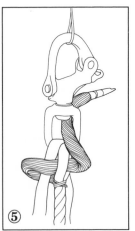

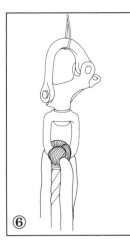

⑤ Finish the crown by passing #3 *away* from you, through the eye of the shackle.

⑥ Draw the Crown Knot up fairly snug.

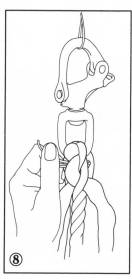

⑦ Take any strand and begin tucking over 1 and under 1 against the lay (from left to right, with shackle upmost). Leave the Constrictor in place for the moment.

⑧ When all 3 strands have been tucked once, carefully cut the Constrictor with the point of a sharp knife or scissors and remove the twine. Fair the splice, drawing on each strand in turn until crown and tucks are optimally compact.

⑨ Continue tucking for at least 4 full tucks. Roll firmly between your hands or underfoot for a final fairing. Either cut the ends off a rope diameter in length and allow them to wear off in use or whip or tie a Constrictor over the last tuck before cutting the ends flush.

Double-Braid Eye Splice

D ouble-braid rope comprises a braided cover around an independent
braided core. Double-braid splicing, in essence, goes like this: The core
sneaks out of the side of the cover, a short ways down the standing part; the
core then grabs the end of the cover and is pulled back into the standing part,
taking the cover with it and forming the eye. That's it.

It's a bizarre, alien construction, and one that most people initially find
intimidating. But the basic idea is very, very simple—simpler structurally
than the Three-Strand Eye Splice. Most of the following instructions are just
details that help the splice come out optimally smooth and strong.

The Double-Braid Splice, unlike the Three-Strand, always requires special
tools. The "fid and pusher" tools originally developed for this job are still
widely used, but are losing ground to a new generation of cheap, versatile,
fast, alternatives. The instructions here will work no matter what tools you
use; the illustrations show Fid-O's ingenious Super Snake.

Although the structure is simple, a Double-Braid Eye Splice involves a lot
of picky details to make the splice easier to manipulate and to help it come
out optimally smooth and strong. Some extra-hard-laid ropes will require
still pickier details. Others may have a straight or twisted core instead of a
braided one. For these exotic lines, consult manufacturers' and toolmakers'
instructions. But practice this splice first; the others are all variations on it.

There is no practical equivalent to the Shackle Splice in double-braid rope,
but since the double-braid flattens out over a shackle better than the three-
strand, one can often get away without a thimble if the loads are not extreme.
Also, there are shackles available with wide-radius bows, to distribute load
better. Still, keep an eye out for chafe; most of double-braid's strength is in
the cover.

① For a few practice splices, get about 20 feet of 1/2-inch braided nylon. If the ends are fused, wrap them lightly with electrical tape and cut the fused bits off.

The 1st step is to put reference marks on the cover (outer braid). With a felt-tip pen, make the 1st mark 24 diameters from the end. In this case that's 24 × 1/2 inch, or 12 inches. The core will attach to the cover at this mark, and all of the cover below this mark will be drawn into the standing part of the rope.

To make it easier to draw the cover in, you'll be tapering it. Mark for the taper now by counting down 5 pairs of yarns from the 1st mark. Mark the 5th pair, and the matching pair next to it, forming a little chevron. Count down 4 pairs further and make another chevron, just like the 1st. Continue, marking every 5th pair, then every 4th, to the end.

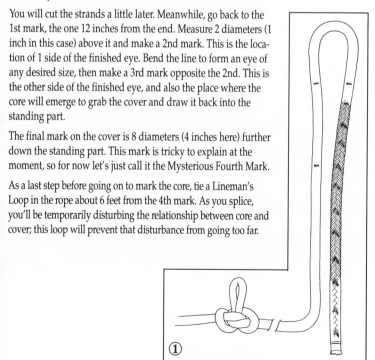

You will cut the strands a little later. Meanwhile, go back to the 1st mark, the one 12 inches from the end. Measure 2 diameters (1 inch in this case) above it and make a 2nd mark. This is the location of 1 side of the finished eye. Bend the line to form an eye of any desired size, then make a 3rd mark opposite the 2nd. This is the other side of the finished eye, and also the place where the core will emerge to grab the cover and draw it back into the standing part.

The final mark on the cover is 8 diameters (4 inches here) further down the standing part. This mark is tricky to explain at the moment, so for now let's just call it the Mysterious Fourth Mark.

As a last step before going on to mark the core, tie a Lineman's Loop in the rope about 6 feet from the 4th mark. As you splice, you'll be temporarily disturbing the relationship between core and cover; this loop will prevent that disturbance from going too far.

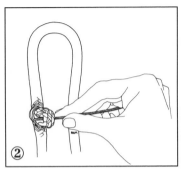

② The cover is all marked; time to turn your attention to the core. With an awl, sail needle, or other pointy tool, gently nudge open a hole in the cover at the 3rd mark, so that you can see the core inside. With the point of the tool, scoop a bight of the core right out of the cover. Be very careful to avoid snagging any cover yarns or leaving behind any core yarns.

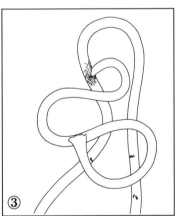

③ Pull the entire end of the core out at the 3rd cover mark . . .

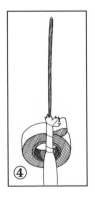

④ . . . and attach your splicing tool to it with a smooth, very tight wrapping of electrical tape. In the same manner, attach another splicing tool to the cover now as well.

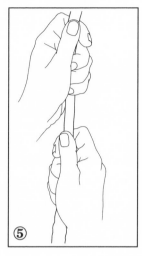

⑤

⑤ Now you need to make a reference mark on the core at the point where it exits the cover. But in extracting the core you invariably pull some slack into the cover. So anchor the standing part of the rope, on the far side of the Loop Knot, to something solid. Then take hold of the standing part on the end side of the Loop Knot and, using both hands, milk any slack towards the end.

⑥ When all slack is out of the cover, make a mark on the core just where it exits the cover.

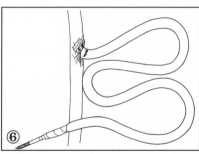

⑥

⑦ Slide the cover back from this mark, exposing more core. Make a 2nd mark 12 diameters (6 inches) away from the end. This is where the cover will attach to the core. The 12 diameters' distance from the exit point is sufficient to draw the cover far enough into the standing part when the splice is done. Make a final mark about 30 diameters from the 2nd.

Pick up the cover and thread it into the core at the 2nd mark on the core, pointed towards the 3rd mark.

Note: If you are splicing the eye through a halyard shackle, you must thread the cover through the shackle before this step.

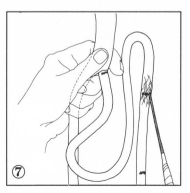

⑦

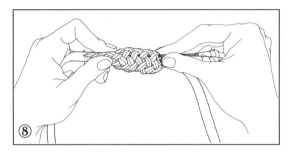

⑧ Bunch the core up ahead of the tool to create a roomy cage for it to travel in. It is extremely important to avoid snagging any core yarns with the tool as you thread the cover in.

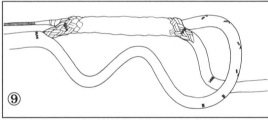

⑨ Exit the tool at the 3rd mark on the core. Pull the cover through until the 1st mark on the cover emerges.

⑩ The cover is now attached to the core. You've pulled it through extra far in order to expose the portion of the cover you're going to taper.

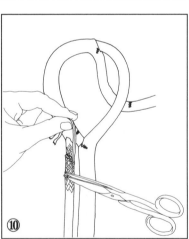

Remove the splicing tool from the cover. With the point of a pair of scissors, gently raise a small bight in a pair of marked yarns. Cut this bight, then pull on the *end* half of the cut pair, to pull those 2 yarns right out of the end. You'll have to pull firmly at first, but it will get easier as you work towards the end.

Repeat with each pair of marked yarns. You should end up with a gently tapering end. If you didn't, you miscounted when you made your marks. Start over.

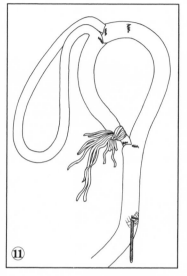

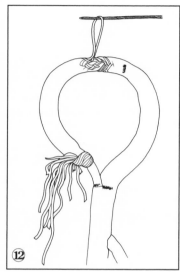

⑪ The cover is tapered. Now you want to withdraw it far enough to expose the 1st mark on the cover at the point where the cover went into the core. But you don't want the end of the cover to disappear into the core; not yet. To prevent this, make a Half-Hitch around the core with the end of the cover. Then pull the cover back, bunching the core up against the Half-Hitch.

Pick up the core end and thread it into the cover at the 1st mark on the cover, pointing away from the Half-Hitch. Thread along, bunching up the cover ahead of the tool to avoid snags. When you reach the "throat" of the eye, keep going, but be doubly cautious to avoid snagging, as you must work the tool along between core and cover here. Exit the tool at the Mysterious Fourth Mark, and pull the core out after it. The 4th mark is there to give the core sufficient "bury," so that it is gripped, Chinese-handcuff-style, in the finished splice.

⑫ The cover has gone into the core, and the core into the cover. They intersect at a point called the *crossover*. By binding core and cover against each other at this point, you make a tight, compact crossover. By gently milking core and cover away from the crossover, you also make it smooth. The crossover will be drawn into the standing part soon, so it mustn't be bulky or lumpy or it won't fit.

It also mustn't slip apart in service, or the entire splice could come undone. To "lock" the crossover, pull a yarn out of the core end at the crossover. Pull only on the *end* side, or you will distort the standing part of the core.

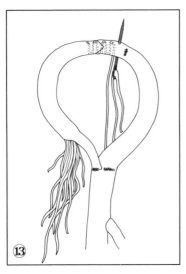

⑬ Thread this core yarn onto a sail needle and stitch back and forth a few times. Trim the end flush.

Untie the Half-Hitch in the cover end. Milk away from the crossover, towards the cover end. The end will disappear inside the core.

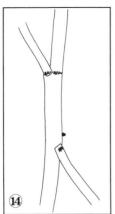

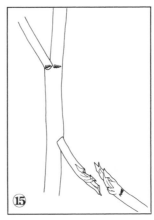

⑭ Milk away from the crossover, towards the core end. Milk all slack out of the cover, right down to where the core end emerges. Mark the core where it exits the cover.

⑮ Pull the core out a short ways, then cut it on a long diagonal above the mark. This gives the core a quick taper. Once more, milk away from the crossover towards the core end. This time the core will disappear inside the cover.

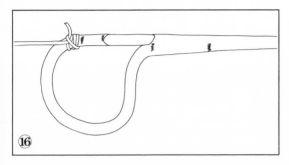

16 Core and cover are interlinked and trapped inside each other. There is slack in the standing part of the cover, and it only remains to milk that slack towards the crossover, to draw the eye down to its desired size. This will be easier to do if the crossover side of the eye is under tension, since a line under tension gets thinner, and so will fit more readily into the hole in the cover.

So if you've detached the rope's standing part from the solid object after step 5, reattach it now. Next, tie a line of about 1/4-inch diameter to the eye with a Camel Hitch (page 31), just above the 2nd mark on the cover. Attach this line to a tackle or come-along and pull taut. This will tension the core only.

Starting at the Loop Knot, milk the cover firmly towards the crossover. Keep working at it until the 1st and 3rd marks on the cover are next to each other.

The amount of slack in the cover at the beginning of this step is determined by the position of the 2nd mark on the core. Attaching the cover to the core at that point effectively shortens the core, creating slack in the cover. After the 1st and 3rd marks are lined up, there will probably still be some slack in the cover. So to finish the splice, undo the Loop Knot and milk the cover very firmly the whole length of the line. Do this even if there is no apparent slack in the cover, as core and cover often come from the factory unevenly tensioned, which reduces rope strength.

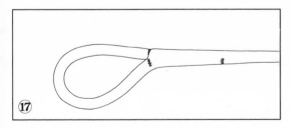

17 The finished splice.

CHAIN SPLICES

M *any vessels have anchor chains that are part chain, part rope. The two parts are commonly joined by shackling a thimbled eye-splice to the chain. This makes a bulky, clumsy joint that hangs up on roller, chock, and, worst of all, on the anchor capstan or windlass. To compound things, a shackle pin that will fit into the end link of chain usually belongs to a shackle that is weaker than the chain—it is a built-in weak link. And finally, the thimble can get sideways in the stretchy nylon eye, causing chafe that can eat clear through the rope.*

The Shackle Splice (pages 91–93) is usually not an option here, since the chain's links are normally too small to accomodate all three strands of rope of the appropriate size.

But there are two thimbleless, shackleless alternatives. The first of these, the Three-Strand, Single-Link Chain Splice, requires a bit of skill and some hair-spiking gel, but is easily the more compact and neat of the two. It is obviously for three-strand rope only. The second, the Shovel Splice, is for either three-strand or double-braid.

Note: See rope and chain manufacturers' specifications to match strength. There are several grades of chain of varying tensile strength, and three-strand and braided rope of the same diameter have different tensile strengths as well.

Three-Strand, Single-Link Chain Splice

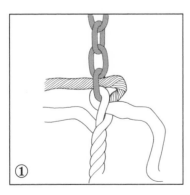

① Soak about 3 feet of the end of the rope with hair-spiking gel, and let dry. Unlay about 2 feet of the rope and thread 2 of the ends together through the last link of chain. With the 1st end, make a counterclockwise loop, end behind the standing part, and draw up snug. Draw the 2nd end (shaded strand) up snug beside the 1st.

② Begin unlaying the 3rd strand (the one that did not go through the link) and laying the 2nd strand into the space it vacates. This is the same procedure as that used for the Three-Strand Mending Splice (pages 105–106). Continue laying the 2nd strand in until it has about 6 inches of end remaining, then knot the 2 ends together, left over right, and tuck the 2 ends over and under against the lay for 4 tucks each.

③ Return to the 1st end. Tuck it over and under, against the lay, 4 or 5 times.

④ The finished splice, with a Double Constrictor holding the rope snug against the last link to prevent chafe.

Shovel Splice

I f the rope portion of your anchor rode is double-braid, or if it is three-strand but you don't feel like fussing your way through the Three-Strand, Single-Link Chain Splice, this is the chain splice for you. It involves separating the rope end into four equal-size bundles and weaving them into the chain. Two go back and forth through the links in one plane, two go up and down, through the links in the other plane.

After a sufficient number of tucks for security, the splice is covered with Double Constrictors, drawn very tight. This is a redundant-security alternative to the usual practice of "serving" (wrapping the splice with a single length of twine).

This is called the Shovel Splice because if it gets in the mud, it tends, because of its loose fibers, to bring up lots of mud with it.

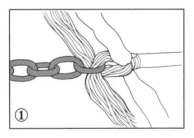

① Apply a very snug Double Constrictor to the rope about 15-18 inches from the end. Separate the yarns into 4 equal-size bundles and tape the ends. Pass 2 opposite bundles through the 1st link, in opposite directions. Draw up and fair, so that all yarns are taking an even strain.

② Pass the other 2 bundles through the next link, in opposite directions. Draw up and fair. Continue tucking alternate pairs of bundles through alternate links, tucking each pair at least 6 times.

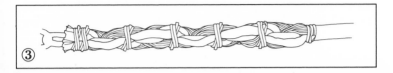

③ The finished splice, with several Double Constrictors along its length, and 2 Double Constrictors to secure the ends, which are cut off nearly flush.

Three-Strand Mending Splice

*W*hen a line becomes severely chafed or receives an accidental nick, it is often only one strand that receives most or all of the damage. The Three-Strand Mending Splice is a temporary repair for that damage. It does not restore the rope to like-new strength, but it does make it usable until you have the opportunity to reeve a new line. And it does so without the block-clogging bulkiness of the Short Splice, and with only negligible reduction in line length.

To keep the mending strand from losing its lay, get out the hair-spiking gel you used for the Three-Strand, Single-Link Chain Splice. With or without the gel, you'll need care and skill here, so that the mending strand will share load evenly with its neighbors.

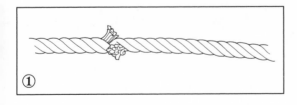

① For easiest handling, prepare the line by soaking it in hair-spiking gel (available at drugstores) for about 18 inches on either side of the damaged area. Soak a 2-foot length at 1 end of a line of identical size, material, and construction. You will be removing the mending strand from this 2nd line.

Sever the damaged strand, being careful to avoid cutting the other 2 strands.

② Remove a 2-foot-long strand from the 2nd line mentioned above. Begin unlaying 1 of the severed ends. Set the middle of the mending strand into the resulting vacant space.

③ Continue to unlay the severed end, laying the mending strand in behind it. Set it in firmly; it should be indistinguishable from the other 2 strands.

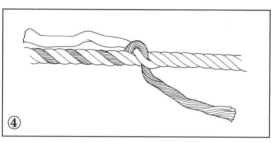

④ When there are about 6 inches of the mending strand remaining, secure it to the severed strand with a Half Knot, left over right, and draw up.

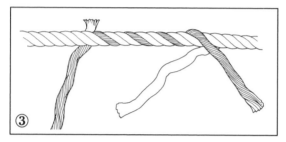

⑤ Begin tucking the 2 strands, as for an Eye Splice, over 1, under 1, against the lay.

⑥ Make 4 full tucks, 5 for nylon. Fair and trim as for an Eye Splice. Repeat the procedure with the other 2 ends.

Mending Splice for Braid

This is really more of a darn than a splice. With a sail needle you weave a length of yarn (taken from a scrap piece of similar rope) into the chafed or cut area. Be sure to overlap the damaged area considerably, so the darning thread is firmly anchored in sound rope.

If the core is also damaged, it can be worthwhile to extrude that section—as in the Double-Braid Eye Splice, but without withdrawing the end—and darn it first. Core and cover need to move independently of each other when passing over sheaves, so avoid snagging the core when darning the cover.

This mending splice represents a simple darning job, but with real structural significance.

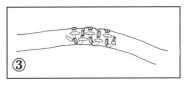

① Thread a sail needle with unwaxed twine. A yarn taken from a piece of rope similar to the one you're mending is ideal.

Begin weaving the needle under, over, under into the cover in the damaged area. Be careful to avoid snagging the core.

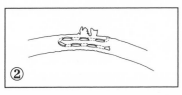

② Continue mending, extending your stitches well into whole rope on either side of the damaged area.

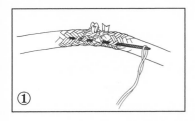

③ Finish with stitches made at right angles to the 1st stitches. Stick the needle once through the entire rope, then cut the twine flush.

Three-Strand Short Splice

J ust as an Eye Splice is a stronger, multistrand alternative to the Bowline, so a Short Splice is a stronger, multistrand alternative to a Bend.

Many eyes are permanent, so it doesn't usually matter that Eye Splices can't be untied. But most bends are temporary, and that is why the Short Splice isn't used much, despite its superior strength. It is generally used as a repair knot for severed lines, but even in that application its usefulness is limited to jobs in which its bulk won't have to try to wedge its way through blocks and fairleads ("Three-Strand Mending Splice," pages 105–106).

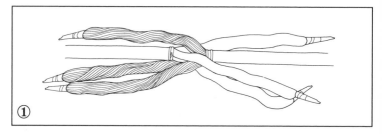

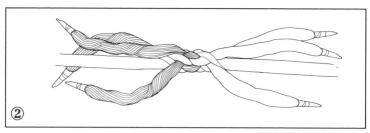

① Tie a Constrictor, and milk and tape the ends of both lines, as for a Three-Strand Eye Splice (page 86). Join the 2 ends together so that each strand lies between 2 opposing strands.

② Tuck each strand of both ends once, over 1 and under 1 against the lay. Remove the Constrictor, then draw up any slack.

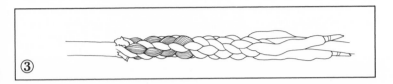

③

③ Continue tucking, fairing after each row of tucks. Tuck each set 3 or 4 times for natural fibers and coarse synthetics, at least 5 times for nylon and other slick synthetics. Trim the ends after the final fairing. Whip or Constrictor over the last tuck for extra security.

Double-Braid Short Splice

T his is a light-duty and/or emergency method for joining two ends of double-braid rope without an objectionable increase in diameter. The splice will fit through most blocks and fairleads that plain rope will fit through.

This splice can reduce rope strength by 20 percent or so; do not subject it to extremes of loading. Ashore, it is useful to make up slings for moving pipe, logs, etc., provided that the rope is sufficiently large to compensate for the weakness of the knot. Afloat, one excellent application is for the endless furling line required for some roller-furling staysail systems.

If you use the Double-Braid Short Splice to repair a parted halyard or sheet, reduce tension accordingly.

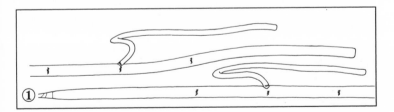

①

① Mark each cover at 24, 36, and 48 diameters from the end. Make a Loop Knot in each cover about 6 feet beyond the 3rd mark, as for the Double-Braid Eye Splice (page 95).

Extract the core from each line at the 2nd mark and mark each core at the point it emerges, again as for the Double-Braid Eye Splice.

Apply a splicing tool to each cover end.

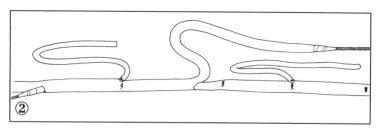

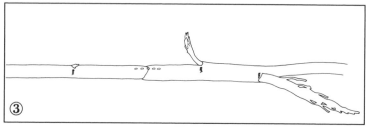

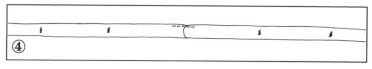

② Insert one cover into the other at the 1st mark. Bring the end out at the 3rd mark. Repeat with the other cover. Be careful to avoid snagging any core or cover yarns.

③ Pull covers in opposite directions to tighten the crossover. Smooth the crossover by milking away from it to either side, without pulling it apart. Stitch the crossover securely with a length of stout, unwaxed Dacron twine.

Mark the covers where they exit at the 3rd marks. Pull each one out and cut it in a rough taper above the mark you just made. Pull the cores out and cut them in a rough taper above their exit-point marks.

Finish by milking all slack out so that cores and covers withdraw into the rope.

Note: If no increase in diameter can be tolerated, cut the tapers starting at 10 diameters above the exit-point marks.

④ Stitch through the rope at the 3rd marks to hold the cores in place. Undo the loops and milk any slack towards the ends. This is the finished splice.

CHAPTER SEVEN

BELAYS

A Belay is much more than a Hitch made around a cleat. A Belay is a dynamic act, a way of securing and adjusting tension under any load the line can bear. Cleats, pins, and other belaying fixtures are the highly evolved tools that make this dynamic act possible, but only if your method of belaying is equally evolved.

In the following instructions, you will note that all good Belays have certain characteristics in common: the line comes into the Belay at an angle, to prevent jamming; the Belay starts with a turn, for positive control; the minimum number of crossing turns needed for complete security are added to the first turn; and all of the Belays are structured so that they can be "surged," that is, they allow you to play out slack at a controlled rate, regardless of load.

Belay to Cleat

C leats work best when they're scaled to the size of line belayed to them. A rule of thumb is to have an inch of cleat length for every sixteenth of an inch of line diameter. Thus a half-inch-diameter line goes onto an eight-inch cleat.

Be sure that the cleat is solidly made and solidly bolted in place; a flimsy or lightly fastened cleat can be major trouble. And inspect all cleats for line-chafing sharp edges or nicks. A few minutes with a file will fix most problems.

When belaying to anything but a bollard, always remember: far end first. That is, the line should come at the cleat at a twenty- to thirty-degree angle and touch the end **away** *from the load first. This prevents the line from jamming on the cleat and makes it easier to control when surging. If the cleat is not angled to the load, make your turn around the far end anyway, and take extra care when casting off.*

When casting off from a cleat or any other Belay, remove the turns deliberately, feeling for any strain on the end. There might well be more load on the standing part than you realize, and carelessly cast-off lines can easily get away from you.

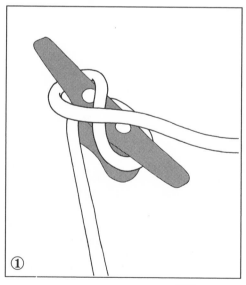

① The line leads to the cleat at a 20-30 degree angle, touching the *far end* first. Make a turn around the base of the cleat, then commence making figure-8 turns.

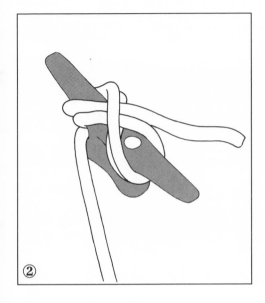

② After 2 figure-8 turns, slip a Half-Hitch over the end of the cleat. Note that the Hitch shown continues the pattern of the figure-8 turns.

Note: With very slick line under heavy load, it may be necessary to add more figure-8 turns before making the Hitch.

Belay to Pin

The belaying pin used to be the dominant belaying fixture afloat. Pins are easier to make than cleats, and are arguably more versatile and easier to belay to than cleats. But they and the rail they sit in take up a lot of room, which is in short supply on most modern boats. And it's hard to design pins and rails to take today's extreme loads.

Nevertheless, pins are often handy, mounted in sheer poles between shrouds or "sissy bars" next to the mast, for flag halyards, topping lifts, and other lightly loaded lines. And you can belay halyards to them when in harbor to prevent mast slap. Pins are also still the best way to handle the complexity of lines on traditional craft.

Note that a line can go directly from load to pin, or it can first go through a deck block or "sweat hook." These arrangements allow you to apply more tension on the line, and they reduce the load on the pin. Another load-sharing strategy is to take a turn around one pin, then belay it to the pin next to it.

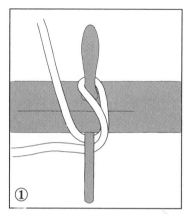

① When the line leads to the pin from above, take it to the bottom of the pin first. Bring the line straight up and make a turn around the top of the pin. (Note that the line comes to the pin at an angle. This and the first non–figure-8 turn prevent jamming under load and prevent the pin from spinning in its hole.)

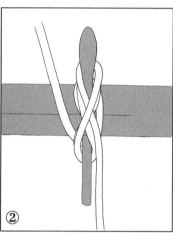

② Make 2 figure-8 turns around the bottom and top of the pin and finish with a Half-Hitch around the head of the pin, similar to the finish for Belay to Cleat.

114

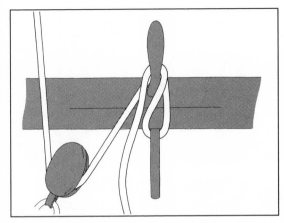

Note: When the line leads to the pin from below, take it to the top 1st then straight down for a turn around the bottom, then make the figure-8 turns (left). For halyards and other heavily loaded lines, share the load between 2 pins, taking a turn over the 1st pin, and belaying to the 2nd (below).

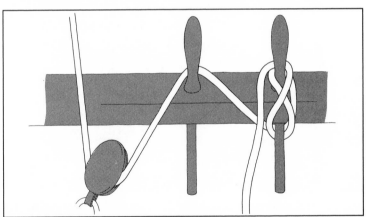

Belay to Bollard

A *bollard is a two-headed belaying fixture. You can take a moderately loaded line to each head with a Capstan Hitch (pages 117–118), or just put a heavily-loaded line around both heads. For the latter, the first turn goes around the **near** head of the bollard; far end first puts excessive leverage on the fastenings holding the fitting in place.*

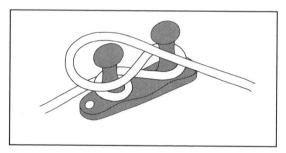

Take a turn around the nearer head of the bollard, then add figure-8 turns around both heads. Finish with a Half-Hitch, as with cleats and belaying pins.

Belay to Winch or Post
CAPSTAN HITCH

Belays are relatively straightforward when you have the horns of a cleat or the ends of a belaying pin to flick turns around. But how do you get an acceptable belay, one than won't twist around and jam, on the featureless circumference of a winch or post? The answer is the Capstan Hitch. It braces the line against itself, and does so under balanced tension.

Extreme loads can cause the rope to chafe itself when surged. You can reduce this problem by taking some extra round turns with the line before beginning the Hitch. You'll need those turns anyway if you use a winch to gain tension before making the Hitch on the winch.

Depending on the load level and the amount of friction between line and winch or post, you may have to help the line around when surging. If you do, just be sure to use your right hand to do the helping (assuming clockwise turns)—your left hand could get drawn into the turns. For the same reason, hold the end well clear of the winch with your left hand.

The line should come into the winch from the load at a five- to ten-degree upward angle to prevent overrides, whether you're belaying, gaining tension, or surging (SEE "Winches," pages 150–152).

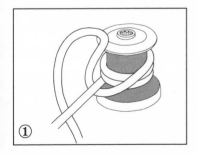

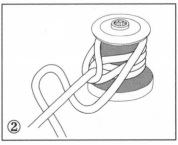

① Make 2 or 3 turns around the winch to control the load while belaying. Lead a bight of the end under the standing part. Without twisting it, drop this bight over the winch.

② Pull the first bight snug, then form a 2nd bight on the other side of the standing part, and drop this over the winch.

117

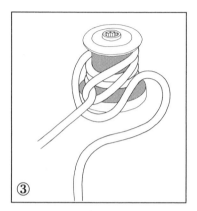

③ Pull the 2nd bight snug, and once again lead a bight under the standing part. For heavily loaded, slippery lines, drop this bight, too, over the winch and haul taut. For most situations, tie a Half-Hitch with this bight around the standing part to finish.

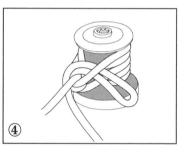

④ The finished belay, with 2 bights over the winch and a Half-Hitch around the standing part. Regardless of the number of bights on the winch, always finish with a Half-Hitch.

CHAPTER EIGHT

COILING

I f you think of rope in use as an electrical current, then coiled rope is a battery—potential energy, waiting to be used. You want to be able to tap that energy instantly, and you can't do that without careful coiling and securing of the coil. Partly this involves plain old tidiness, but partly it involves understanding the materials you're working with.

For example, there is an ancient stricture always to coil clockwise. That is, the coil, as you are facing it, always has rope added to it in a clockwise circle. But it turns out that this only makes sense with right-laid rope, and it is done in order to have the coil "run free," without kinks or hockles: When you coil you give the rope a slight twist so that it lays flat. This twist is also clockwise, so that it causes the lay of the rope to open up a bit with each turn. When the rope runs it untwists, and the lay closes back up again.

If you were to coil counterclockwise you'd be *tightening* the lay with those twists, and the twists would not go away when the rope ran.

There are a number of other techniques to neutralize twists, some specific to "layless" modern line. Studying when and why to use them is a good way to get to know the ropes.

Coiling Three-Strand
CLOCKWISE

H old the coil in either your left or right hand, whichever you prefer. Just be sure to coil clockwise. Note that the same twists that open up the lay of the coiled line, enabling it to lie flat, tighten the lay of the standing part that remains to be coiled. Therefore, shake out any excess twists as you go. If you coil towards the belay, the twists in the standing part can't be shaken out. That's why you should always coil *away* from the belay with this method.

Very large coils need to be made on the deck. Since you'll be working towards the end, the standing part will be on the bottom of the coil when you're done. This is a problem, since the standing part needs to run when you put the line to use again, and it can't with the whole coil sitting on top of it. So when you're done coiling on the deck, carefully flip the whole works over, to get the standing part on top. A coil that is to be hung up should have the end on the outside when secured. That way when it's time to put the line to work you simply drop the coil "face down" on the deck, leaving the standing part free to run.

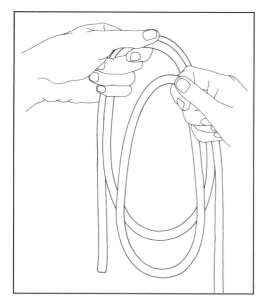

Start with the end in one hand, hanging down about 2 feet. Begin making even sized, clockwise turns with your other hand, placing each turn into the 1st hand. Twist the line clockwise slightly with each turn, so that the turns lie flat. The end should hang below the turns so it cannot become tangled in them.

Note: This illustration shows the coil being made in the left hand, but many people prefer to make it in the right hand. In either hand the turns are made clockwise.

Coiling Over and Under

Because the yarns in braided line run in both directions, there is no lay to open up and absorb the twists that are generated by standard three-strand coiling. That's why braided line is best coiled "over and under:" one turn is made in standard fashion and twists the line one way, and a subsequent "hitch" turn twists it the other. The opposing twists neutralize each other, so the line can run free. This is also the technique to use for wire rope, garden hose, electrical cable, or any other stubborn coilable material. It's even a good technique to use with stiff three-strand rope.

Warning: Always leave the end hanging *below* the finished coil. If it gets passed through the middle of the coil, it will automatically tie a long and frustrating series of Overhand Knots.

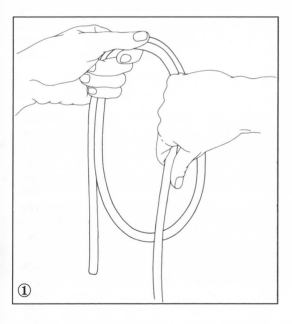

① Begin with a clockwise turn, as for a regular 3-strand clockwise coil.

Pick up the 2nd turn with your hand inverted.

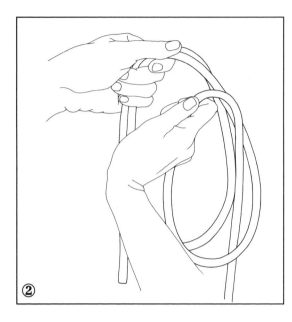

② Turn your hand over, forming a loop. Place this loop in the 1st hand. Make another regular clockwise turn, then another loop, and so on.

Note: Because the twists are neutralized, you can coil towards the belay with this technique.

Figure-Eight Coiling
IN HAND

*L*ike *Over-and-Under Coiling, Figure-Eight Coiling is a way to neutralize twists. In this case, you twist one way at the bottom of the loop and the other way at the top. Try both methods and see which you prefer.*

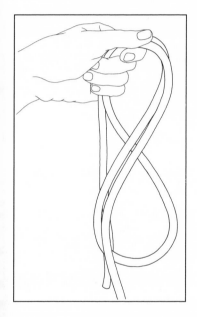

Make a series of Figure-Eight turns on your hand. Keep the turns lying flat by twisting one way at the bottom, the other way at the top. For extra-long lines, this coil can also be made on the ground or deck.

Figure-Eight Coiling
ON DECK

For coiling very long lines you can use any coil technique on the deck instead of trying to cram the entire heavy, unwieldy thing onto your hand.

The Figure-Eight Coil made on the deck is a particularly good way to prepare for running the very long halyards on gaff- and square-riggers, since it is virtually snarl-proof, even during high-speed running, so long as the lead is upward.

This coil is made **towards** the belay, so that the coil need not be turned over before running. It can be made this way because, like the Over-and-Under, it generates no leftover twists.

BAGGING

The practice of stuffing lines into bags instead of coiling them is relatively recent. Bagging is a way of keeping twists out of lines, but one mostly sees it as an expedient aboard racing craft and other vessels that have all their lines leading to the cockpit. Bagging presents a way of dealing with a whole bunch of strings that are all spilling into the busiest area of the boat.

CHAPTER NINE

SECURING A COIL

Securing on a Pin or Cleat
TWISTED BIGHT

O nce a line is belayed and coiled, you need some way of securing it to keep it out of traffic and tangle-free until it is called upon again. With often-used lines such as sheets, this can simply mean letting the coil lay in an untravelled spot. But with most lines you have to get the coils off the deck.

The most common method of securing is to hang the coil on the cleat or pin to which it is belayed, with a Twisted Bight. The coil's circumference should be such that it hangs clear of the deck when secured. The end should be on the outside, so that when you want to use the line, you just drop the coil on the deck, face down, leaving the standing part free to run.

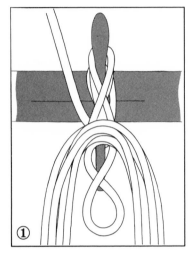

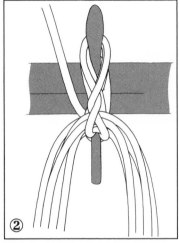

① Coil the line, and leave about 1 foot of standing part between the coil and the pin. Hold the coil close to the pin and this length of standing part will fold, forming a bight. Reach through the coil to grasp this bight, and twist it a full turn counter-clockwise. Bring the twisted bight up through the coil and drop it on to the pin.

② The secured coil.

Securing on a Pin or Cleat
ROUND TURN MADE WITH THE BIGHT

W hen secured with a twisted bight, the lay of three-strand rope opens a bit, much as it does when it is coiled. And once again braided rope, particularly stiff halyard stuff, resists the twist, just as it does with coiling. In this circumstance, secure the coil to its cleat or pin with a round turn made with the bight. This technique is also handy for very stiff three-strand rope.

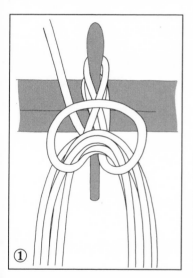

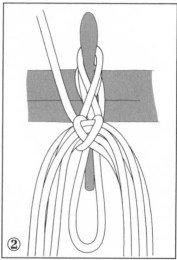

① Coil the line and leave about 1 1/2 feet of standing part between the coil and the pin. Hold the coil close to the pin, causing the length of standing part to fold into a bight. Reach through the coil and bring this bight up . . .

② . . . and over the top of the coil, then down behind the coil, on the right side of the standing part, and once again up through the coil. The bight may form a twist of its own accord. This is OK. Drop the bight over the pin.

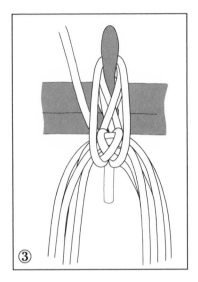

③ The secured coil.

Gasket Hitch

I f a line is belayed with a rope clutch, there might be no cleat or pin to
hang the coil on. And some cleats are so small that there's not enough
room on them for both a secure belay and a coil-securing bight. And then
there are mooring lines and other medium-length lines that need to be stowed
out of the way when not in use. The best stow for all of these needs is a
Gasket Hitch.

Like the Twisted Bight, the Gasket Hitch can be made with the bight
between the coil and the belay. It can also be made with an end for lines that are
to be stowed off deck. The Gasket Hitch is simple to tie and very secure, making
it an alternative to securing a coil with a Twisted Bight in storm conditions.

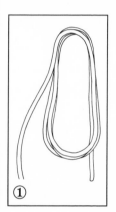 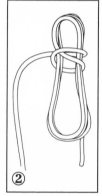 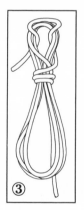 

① Coil up all but the last 3 to 4 feet of a line.

② Holding on to the head of the coil in 1 hand, begin making horizontal turns around
the coil with the end in your other hand. Looking down from the top of the coil, these
turns are made clockwise. Make several turns, working towards the head of the coil.

③ Push a bight of the end through the head of the coil. Open up this bight and drop it
down over the head of the coil until it rests on top of the turns. Pull on the end to draw
up.

④ The finished coil. The Gasket Hitch can be made on Clockwise, Over-and-Under, or
Figure-Eight coils (SEE chapter 8).

Quick Turn

A short-term stow for often-used lines, the Quick Turn won't stay put as well as the Gasket Hitch, but it is indeed much quicker. It holds together best when hung up by its built-in bight. Ashore or afloat, it's a great stow for extension cords as well as rope.

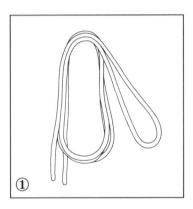

① Coil up all but the last 3 to 4 feet of line. Make a long bight with the end and lay this bight over your coil-holding hand.

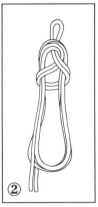

② Pass the bight clockwise (when viewed from the top of the coil) around the coil horizontally. After 1 complete turn, stick the bight through the head of the coil, above the horizontal turn. Pull on the bight to draw up.

Toggled Coil

A very long line, such as a gaff halyard, can make for a huge coil when the sail is up: It's not uncommon to have over two hundred feet to deal with. For a coil of this size, a toggle and eye, seized to a shroud or rail, is by far the handiest stow.

The toggle can be a piece of wood you've whittled, a rope button, even a large washer knotted into the end of the line.

A Toggled Coil is easy to apply, tidy, and it releases instantly.

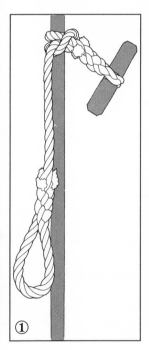

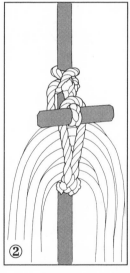

① Crown Splice (see pages 91–93) a toggle into one end of a short piece of rope. The toggle can be a dowel or section of broom handle, with a groove cut in its middle. In the other end of the rope, splice an eye big enough to fit readily over the toggle. Clove Hitch the rope to a stay, pole, etc., above deck.

② To hang a coil, bring the eye up through the head of the coil and button the eye on the toggle.

Stoppered Coil

F or long-term stowage, particularly of very long pieces of rope, stopper the coil. This is simply a matter of making a series of seizings around the coil, so that the turns can't get fouled while the coil reposes in the lazaret.

To make a coil more compact, first stopper the perimeter, then half-twist the coil, fold it over onto itself, and seize the two halves together. A Figure-Eight Coil may be simply folded in half after stoppering.

A Stoppered Coil is also the stow for unknottable items such as garden hose and wire rope.

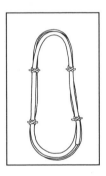

Coil a line and lay it down on deck or on the ground. Tie 4 to 6 pieces of twine about its circumference with a Constrictor or a round turn and Square Knot (page 82).

Self-Stoppered Coil

T his is a way of stoppering a coil with its own ends. Not quite as firmly in control as true stoppering, it is adequate for small- to medium-sized coils, provided you don't kick them around too much.

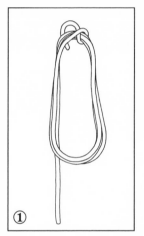

① Coil a line. Pass an end around 1 side of the coil, then form a Hitch by passing it up between the coil and the last turn.

② Pass the end around once more. Bring it up over the last turn, then under its own part, to form a 2nd Hitch. Repeat with the other end, on the opposite side of the coil.

Heaving-Line Trigger

O rdinarily, heaving-lines are coiled, then held in one hand, much as one might hold a bicycle tire, and thrown underhand or sidearm. The trouble is that it's very easy to snag the coil with your fingers upon release. The result is that the coil does not go where you aimed it.

The Heaving-Line Trigger gives you an easily-held handle and a perfectly controllable release mechanism.

Note that the weight hangs below the coil so that it cannot foul the turns. Note also that the weight is a canvas bag, a soft, nonricocheting alternative to the traditional Monkey's Fist knot.

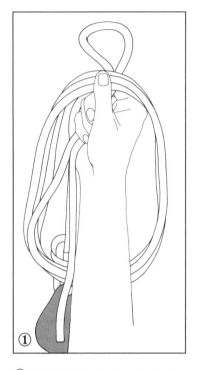

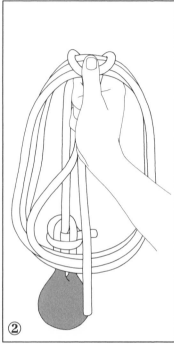

① Coil up the heaving line and hold it so the standing part is on your side of the coil and the heaving-line weight is on the far side.

Make a bight with the standing part and hold it several inches from the end of the bight. Pass the end of the bight through the head of the coil, away from you.

② Fold the bight back towards you, over the top of the coil. Hold it down with your thumb, after removing any slack. The bight should fit snugly around the coil.

You now hold the coil by a "handle." To throw it, make an underhand swing. Release the coil at about chest level by lifting your thumb.

Note that both weight and standing part hang down below coil. In actual use, the standing part would already be tied to a mooring-line eye.

CHAPTER TEN

MECHANICAL ADVANTAGE (Purchase)

R ope is put to work with tension. Sometimes, as with animal tethers and anchor rodes, the load provides its own tension. More often, you must do the work.

Hoisting a dinghy out of the water, or stretching a sail taut, or lifting an engine usually requires more tension than a human being can provide. For these and other high-tension jobs, there are two tools that multiply your strength: blocks and winches.

Blocks multiply your strength by sharing the load with you; the greater the number of turns the line takes through a block or blocks at the load, the greater the share of the load the blocks will bear, and the less force you must provide. The degree of mechanical advantage that a given set of blocks provides is called the "purchase" of that set.

Blocks can vary in efficiency, depending on how much friction the sheave generates as it spins on its axle and rubs against the sides of the block. Very slick modern sheaves will generate friction as low as 2 to 3 percent of the load's weight. Less efficient sheaves might generate 10 percent or more per sheave. Friction is also generated by the rope itself as it passes over the sheave; the bigger the sheave, the less there is of this friction. It pays, therefore, to get the largest, slickest sheaves you can, for ease of hauling.

Winches multiply your strength with leverage. The longer the winch handle and/or the higher the ratio of the internal gearing, the more leverage you have. Winch efficiency is also affected by friction, so look for precise machining, and keep the gears well lubricated.

The more powerful a purchase or winch is, the more slowly it moves the load; in other words, it doesn't make work disappear, it just spreads it out over a longer period of time. In practical terms, greater power also means greater cost and complexity. So the trick in selecting appropriate mechanical advantage is to scale it not only to the job at hand, but to your pocketbook, athletic ability, and how quickly you want the job done.

You could, for example, use a winch with a mechanical advantage of thirty to one to pick up a bale of hay and put it in a pickup truck. It would be an extremely low-effort way to do the job, but also an extremely complicated, expensive, and slow way. It would make much more sense just to pick up the bale and throw it into the truck. But if you had to pick up an engine and move it the same distance, thirty to one would start to sound very attractive. Even then, though, sense would dictate that an exquisite, costly sailboat winch would be less appropriate than the simple, inexpensive winch known as a come-along.

In every instance, you should select the most appropriate tool for the job. In general, move light loads by hand, with no mechanical advantage; move medium loads with the simplest (and thus fastest) block-and-tackle configuration possible; and move heavy loads with a winch, or with a combination of block-and-tackle and winch.

One-Part Purchase

I f you secure a line to a load, run that line up through a block, and then back down to you, you have redirected the lead of the line, but added no mechanical advantage. So to pick up, say, a 120-pound load, you need to pull down with a force of 120 pounds, plus whatever it takes to counteract the effects of sheave friction. You'd have to weigh at least 120 pounds to budge that load, and even then it wouldn't be easy.

However, a one-part purchase can be just the thing for lighter loads, since it enables you to hoist them quickly to any height. A flag halyard is a one-part purchase. And you can send tools and materials up to the roof of a house under construction with a one-part purchase rigged to a scaffold. So when you want to move light loads quickly, you don't need mechanical advantage, just enough rope and a block with one pulley in it, called a single (S) block.

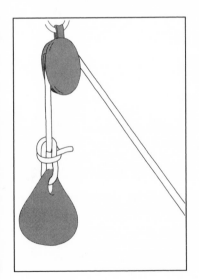

Lead a line up from a load, through a block, and down to yourself. This is a 1:1 mechanical advantage: You can lift a load equal to the force of your downward pull.

Simple Two-Part Purchase

I f you secure a line to something solid overhead, then run the line down, through a single block that is attached to the load, and back up to you, you will have created a two-part purchase. The attachment point overhead takes half the load, and you take half. You can now pick up 120 pounds with a pull of 120/2, or 60 pounds, disregarding friction.

You can't pick up a load very far with this configuration, but it can be handy when you want to put a dolly under a heavy object. Just remember to attach the block above the object's center of gravity, and to keep yourself and everyone else out from under the load.

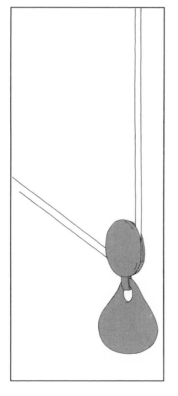

Secure a line overhead, lead it down to a block that is secured to the load, then up to yourself. This is a 2:1 advantage: Since the line overhead shares the load with you, you can lift 2 pounds for every pound of force you exert.

Two-Part Purchase
WITH TURNING BLOCK

T o hoist a load overhead with a two-part purchase, start with the preceding configuration, then lead the line through a block secured overhead, then down to you. As with one-part purchase, this block provides no mechanical advantage; it's a "turning block," there for convenience, not lessened effort.

Many block-and-tackle configurations use a turning block, sometimes more than one, so it can be difficult to determine just what the mechanical advantage is in a given configuration. The trick is to look at the moving block, and count the number of parts of line coming out of it. In this case, the block attached to the load will move when you pull on the line. This block has two parts coming out of it. So you can disregard the overhead block and know for certain that this is a two-part purchase.

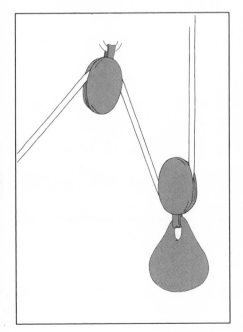

In order to lift a line higher than is practical with a simple 2-part purchase, lead the line up from the block on the load, through a 2nd block secured over-head, then down to yourself. This is still a 2:1 advantage; the 2nd block only re-directs the line, as in a one-part purchase.

Three-Part Purchase

S imply by inverting the previous purchase, putting the single block overhead and a single with becket (an extra attachment point on the block, opposite the bail) on the load, you get a three-part purchase—the moving block has three parts coming out of it. A 40-pound pull will now lift 120 pounds, disregarding friction.

Any block-and-tackle configuration can be inverted in this manner. The more powerful of the two purchases is said to be "rove to advantage." When a purchase is rove to advantage, as this one is, the distance you can move the load is limited by how high above the load you can stand, unless you also use an overhead turning block. So purchases rove to advantage are generally used to move heavy loads short distances.

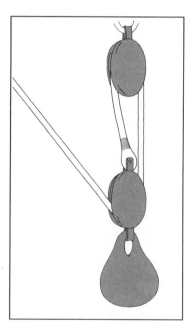

Secure the line to a becket on the block on the load. Lead the line up through a turning block secured overhead, down through the block on the load, then back up to yourself. This is a 3:1 mechanical advantage.

Three-Part Purchase
WITH TURNING BLOCK

This represents the above purchase with a turning block added.

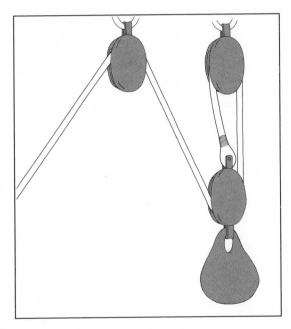

Lead the line up through a 2nd turning block secured overhead, then back down to yourself to allow higher hoisting. This is still a 3:1 advantage.

Three-Part Purchase

WITH DOUBLE BLOCK

Here you combine the two overhead single blocks into one block that has two sheaves, side by side. This is called a double block. The mechanical advantage is still three to one.

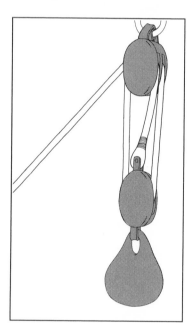

By combining the 2 single turning blocks in the previous figure into a double block, you can gain the convenience of dealing with only 2 blocks, instead of 3.

Four-Part Purchase

FIDDLE

Some double blocks have their sheaves mounted one above the other instead of side by side. One sheave is smaller than the other so that the *lines coming off the two sheaves do not chafe against one another. These blocks are called fiddle blocks.*

In the accompanying illustration, the lower block is a fiddle (F), the upper is a fiddle with becket (FWB). There are four parts coming from the moving block, hence this is a four-part purchase.

If you were to invert this configuration, you would have a five-part purchase.

Triple- and even quadruple-sheave blocks are available for increased mechanical advantage, but that entails reeving more and more rope through increasingly expensive blocks, and moving the load more and more slowly. For these reasons, purchases of a six to one or greater are rare.

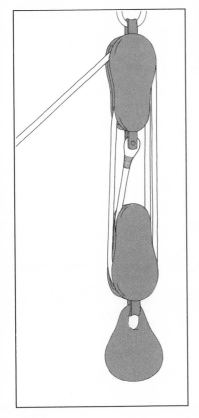

Secure the line to a becket on the upper block. Lead the line down through the smaller sheave on the lower block, up through the smaller sheave on the upper block, down through the larger sheave on the lower block, up through the larger sheave on the upper block, and then down to yourself. This is a 4:1 advantage.

Compound Purchase
3 ON 4

*I*f *you attach a purchase to the hauling part of another purchase, the mechanical advantages of the two are not just added together, they're* multiplied. *This might seem miraculous at first, but remember that any purchase is a power multiplier; a compound purchase is a compound power multiplier.*

In the following illustration, a four-part purchase is compounded by a three-part purchase, for an advantage of twelve to one.

A compound purchase enables you to apply high mechanical advantage using simpler blocks and less rope than an equal-power simple purchase. Hoist length is limited, since the upper compounding block always comes down faster than the load goes up. A winch-and-tackle configuration is another form of compound purchase, often used for main-sheet systems. Ashore, a come-along with a pulley at the load is another form of winch-and-tackle compound purchase. This combination allows full hoisting height.

Note: When employing any compound purchase, it is easy to multiply power so much that you exceed the safe working load on the purchase that is attached to the load; be certain that rope and blocks are scaled to the weight being lifted.

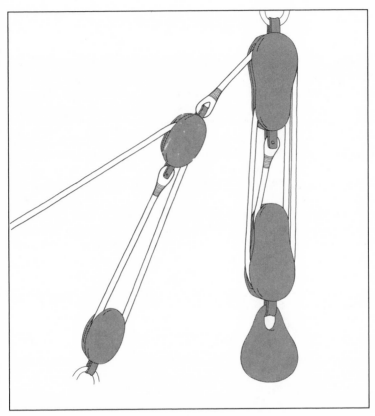

Attach a 4-part purchase (pages 142–43) to the load. Attach the upper block of a 3-part purchase (page 142), inverted, to the hauling part of the 4-part purchase. Attach the lower block of the 3-part purchase to the deck or ground. By pulling on the hauling part of the 3-part purchase, you gain a 12:1 advantage.

Spanish Burton

T he Spanish Burton is an anomaly in both name and structure. In the
following illustration, the block on the left has two parts coming out of it,
so it's a two-part purchase. But wait, one of those two parts is also pulling up
on the block on the right—or is the block on the right pulling down on it?
However you look at it, this interconnected compound purchase has a five-to-
one advantage. And it gets it without having to resort to multisheave blocks.
It's an extremely convenient short-hoist configuration, traditionally used
afloat for bringing dinghies and stores aboard. Ashore, a Spanish Burton is
just the thing for positioning heavy timbers or setting up guys.

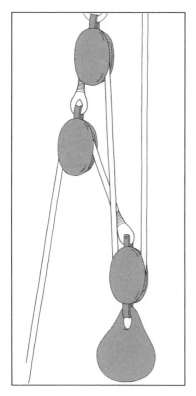

Set up a 2-part purchase with turning
block (page 139). Attach a single block to
the hauling part. Attach a 2nd line to the
becket on the block on the load. Lead this
line up through the single block, and
down to yourself. This is a 5:1 advantage.

TRUCKER'S HITCH

A *Trucker's Hitch is an extemporaneous purchase made by anchoring one end of a line, then passing the other end through a Loop Knot, either in the line's own standing part or in the end of a separate line. No sheaves are involved, so friction is high. But a Trucker's Hitch is a very useful improvised advantage, particularly for lashing loads to truck beds—hence its name—or onto boat decks.*

The slipknot, made as for the Slipknot Bowline (pages 54–56), is the most expedient loop for a Trucker's Hitch, but it will jam under heavy load. Make a Lineman's Loop (pages 63–64), or better yet a Double Lineman's Loop (page 65), if you have the time.

For heavy-duty security, use separate lines, with thimbles spliced in their ends, over the load, and tighten with separate, lighter lines, passed around several times.

A compound mechanical advantage can be gained by "frapping," or pulling sideways on, two adjacent lashings. Frapping is also used to tighten the turns of a Palm-and-Needle Whipping (pages 154–158), or two- and four-leg seizings, (pages 161–64).

Trucker's Hitch
WITH SLIPKNOT

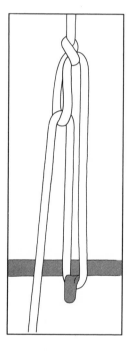

Make a slipknot in the standing part, as for the Slipknot Bowline (pages 54–56). Note that the side of the loop that leads to the end is the sliding part for this knot. Pass the end under a ring, rail, cleat, etc., on the truck bed, then back up and through the loop. This forms a 3-part purchase.

Trucker's Hitch
WITH PENDANTS, FRAPPED

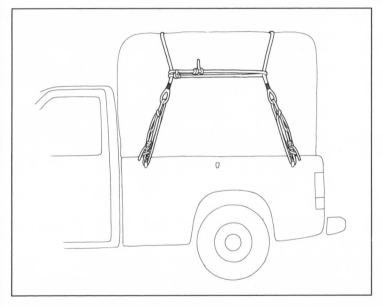

For heavy-duty lashing jobs, splice up 2 pendants, short enough that they don't reach over the load all the way. Use separate lashing lines to pull them taut. In this example, the lashing lines have a Slipknot Trucker's Hitch made in them, for a compound purchase: The line is hitched to the truck bed, and passed through the eye at the end of the pendant. Then a slipknot is formed, as above. The end is passed under a hook or ring on the truck bed, led back up through the slipknot, and finally hauled down and hitched to its own part.

The 2 pendants are further tightened by "frapping": a separate line is hitched to 1 pendant's standing part, led around the other pendant's standing part, back around the 1st pendant, and is hauled taut. It is then Rolling Hitched to its own part.

Winches

SIMPLE

A *winch is a form of lever. Its center, around which the drum and handle rotate, is the fulcrum. In this, the simplest form of winch, mechanical advantage is determined by the difference between handle length and drum radius. The longer the handle is relative to the drum, the greater the mechanical advantage.*

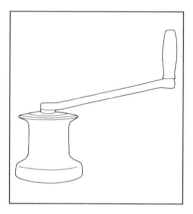

The amount of leverage offered by a winch is determined by the difference between the drum radius and the handle radius. In this instance, the handle radius is 6 times the drum radius, giving a 6:1 advantage.

Winches
GEARED

*I*nternal gearing is another form of lever. In a winch, gearing compounds the handle's leverage. The internal gearing on some winches can be shifted to provide two or even three gearing ratios, like the different gears in a car transmission. The higher gears are for quick takeup or rough adjustments, the lower gears are for heavy loads or fine-tuning.

Tailing a Winch by Hand

*T*ailing a line on a winch is a matter of keeping moderate, even tension on the end of the line as it feeds off the winch, so that the turns of the line around the barrel grip tightly, and don't roll over each other and foul, causing a "wrap."

If possible, one person should tail while another cranks the handle. The tailer simply takes in the slack, hand over hand. If the line begins to slip on the drum as strain comes on, the cranker removes the winch handle so the tailer can very carefully add another turn or two around the barrel.

If you're shorthanded and have to crank and tail by yourself, crank with one hand and tail with the other. You'll need to stop every few turns to reposition your tailing hand.

Note: At no time, whether tailing, adding, or removing turns, should tha tailer's hands get less than six to eight inches from the drum; if the line slips, you'll need room to get your hands clear. This precaution applies no matter how many people are involved in the operation.

Self-Tailing Winch

M *any modern winches come equipped with a "self-tailing" cap on top, which automatically feeds the end off as you crank.*

With self-tailing winches, it is very important that you match line and cap size, to ensure adequate grip on the line, with minimal chafe.

A good self-tailing winch will rarely slip. Still, it's a good idea to always use a human tailer when hauling a crewmember up the mast.

A self-tailing winch has a grooved cap fitted to its top. The rope is gripped in the groove, so no human tailer is required. Matching rope diameter to groove width is crucial for security.

CHAPTER ELEVEN

WHIPPINGS AND SEIZINGS

Whippings and seizings are binding knots, the permanent, heavy-duty cousins to the Constrictor family. A whipping binds together the strands at the end of a line to keep it from ravelling. A seizing binds parts of two or more lines together, so that they act as a unit. Whippings and seizings are structurally similar to one another—another case of "learn one knot, get one free."

There are a number of "modern" alternatives to whippings. These range from glues designed to stick the strands together to the infamous "Butane Backsplice" (fusing the strands with a cigarette lighter). But no one has come up with anything else as secure, soft, durable, and pleasing to eye and hand as a Palm-and-Needle Whipping.

Seizings don't just hold lines together; they're structurally significant, meant to deal with forces that would tear lines apart, or cause them to slide by one another. So always apply seizings with consistent tension, for reliable finished pieces.

PALM-AND-NEEDLE WHIPPING

S imply making a few turns with twine around the end of a line would make a whipping of sorts; a Palm-and-Needle Whipping is an extraordinarily snug, secure, chafe resistant, stitched-together work of art.

The palm is a leather collar that fits around the hand. There is one large hole for the fingers, and a separate hole for the thumb. A dimpled "iron" at the base of the thumb is the most significant part of the palm: brace the butt of a sail needle against this iron, and you can push the needle, painlessly, through the rope. With very little practice, you'll be able to steer the needle exactly where you want it to go.

Palm, needles, and twine are available at any chandlery. But for a little more money you can get a better grade of all three through a sail loft. Ask for a roping palm (left- or right-handed), a few number 13 or 14 needles, and a small spool of their heaviest prewaxed Dacron twine.

The palm can be used not just to push the needle through, but to help you pull each turn taut. The thumb stall is integral to this operation.

The frapping turns of a Three-Strand Whipping settle neatly into the grooves of the rope. If the rope end is chafed, the frapping turns, safe out of harm's way, will hold things together until you can put on another whipping.

But on braided rope there are no groove shelters for frapping turns, so they're the ones that take the chafe. That's why braid whipping involves four frapping turns, protecting in all directions. They also keep the last round turn of the whipping from slipping off the end.

Note that with braid whipping you make your round turns away from the end, whereas with the three-strand whipping the turns go towards the end. If you make your braid-whipping turns towards the end, the hitch that finishes the whipping will end up on the standing-part side, instead of exposed at the end.

Before whipping a braided line, be sure that core and cover are balanced, with no slack in either (SEE "Double-Braid Eye Splice," pages 94–101).

Braid Whipping

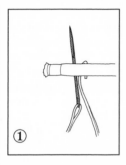 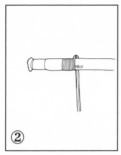 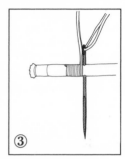

① Middle a fathom (6 feet) of heavy-duty waxed sail twine on a #13 or #14 sailmaker's needle. Anchor the twine near the rope end by stitching through the rope 3 times in a narrow zig-zag pattern, working towards the end. Pull the twine taut.

② Wrap the twine around the rope, making turns away from the end. The turns should be snug, with no spaces between them, and no twists in the twine. Twists stand up and are more likely to chafe.

③ When the turns are a little wider than the rope diameter, stick the needle straight through the rope, right next to the last turn and directly across from where the turns began. Pull snug.

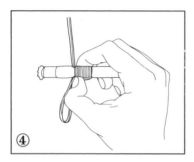

④

④ You have completed the round turns which bind the rope ends. Now begin the frapping turns, which will protect the round turns from chafe.

Lead the needle back across the whipping and stick it straight through the rope, on the end side of the whipping. The needle should emerge where the turns began, at the same point the needle emerges in figure 1.

Before tightening this frapping turn, pull it across the face of the whipping, remove any twists in the section that will lie over the whipping, then pinch this section against the whipping with your thumbnail while you pull the twine taut. This is the surest way to prevent twists in the frapping turns.

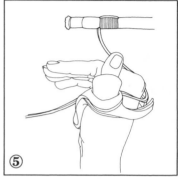

⑤

⑤ Frapping turns need to be hauled extra taut so they will tighten and reinforce the round turns. Pulling hard with bare hands will hurt, but you can wrap the twine around your palm instead.

Start by letting the needle end hang down across the palm of the hand. The standing part lays across the back of the hand. The whipping is about a foot away from the hand.

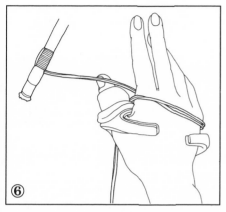

⑥ Reach over the standing part with your fingers. Reach under the standing part with your thumb and rest the standing part of the twine on the leather collar, or "thumb stall" that is built into the palm.

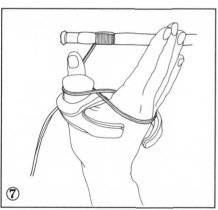

⑦ Rotate your wrist, bringing your thumb back towards you, thus wrapping the twine around the stall. You can now haul the twine hard, and the thumb stall will take most of the load.

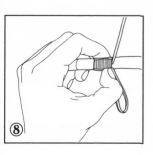

⑧ You are now ready to make another frapping turn. Lead the needle across the whipping again and stick it into the rope directly below the first frapping turn. Angle the needle 45 degrees, so that it emerges midway between the 1st and 2nd frapping turns. Lay the 2nd frapping turn down and pinch it with your thumbnail as before, then wrap the twine around the palm and haul taut.

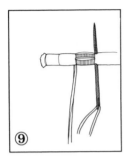

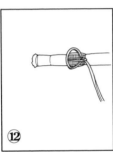

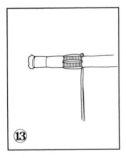

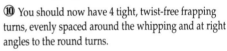

⑨ Lead the needle across the whipping and stick it straight through the rope to form the 3rd frapping turn. Haul taut. Then, as shown here, lead the needle across once more and stick it straight through to form the 4th and final frapping turn. Haul taut.

⑩ You should now have 4 tight, twist-free frapping turns, evenly spaced around the whipping and at right angles to the round turns.

To finish, you'll make a Flat Knot. Start by threading the needle under one of the strands of the frapping turn the needle emerged by. Pull taut.

⑪ Thread the needle under the unoccupied strand of the frapping turn, so that the point emerges between the 2 strands.

⑫ Draw the twine down so that the Flat Knot draws up snugly around the frapping turns.

⑬ Stick the needle straight through the rope once more, and haul to work the Flat Knot down firmly to the base of the whipping. Trim the twine flush, then cut the rope about 1/4 inch from the other end of the whipping.

For insurance, in case this whipping should chafe away, put on a 2nd whipping about 3 rope diameters up the standing part.

Three-Strand Whipping

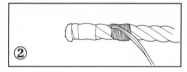

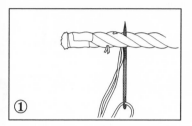

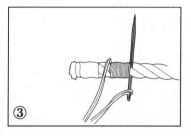

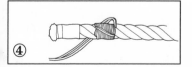

① Anchor the twine by threading it through the rope 3 times in a very short zig-zag pattern, working away from the end. Leave only a slight bit of twine showing on the surface. Bring the needle out between 2 strands after the last pass.

② Wrap the twine around the rope, against the lay, making a whipping about as long as the rope is wide. Make the turns snug, with no spaces between them and no twists in the twine.

When you have sufficient turns, find the groove in which trhe turns started. Trace down this groove to the other end of the whipping. With the end on your left, stick the needle into this groove and out the next groove.

③ Take up all slack in the twine. Trace down the groove in which the twine now sits, to the other end of the whipping. With the end still on the left, stick the needle into this groove and out the next groove. This makes the first frapping turn. Haul this frapping turn tight using the palm, as in the Braid Whipping.

④ The lst frapping turn, hauled taut. Lead the needle along its new groove and . . .

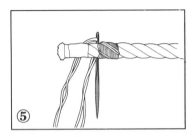

⑤ ... stick the needle into the groove, at the other end of the whipping, end still on the left. Haul taut.

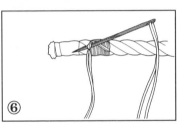

⑥ The needle now emerges where the round turns stopped. The end of the turns forms a little bight of twine around 1 strand. This bight can ride up and come loose; anchor it now by tucking the needle under it, towards the end ...

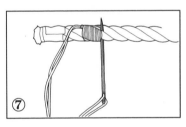

⑦ ... then trace down the last unoccuppied groove. Stick the needle in so that the point emerges at the base of the 1st frapping turn. Haul taut.

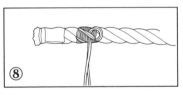

⑧ Pass the needle under the 1st frapping turn. Pull the twine firmly to the bottom of the whipping. This anchors the twine.

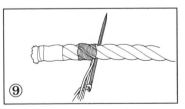

⑨ Finish by sticking the needle once through the rope, right at the base of the whipping. Haul all slack out and trim the twine flush with the rope surface. Cut the rope about 1/8–1/4 inch from the whipping end. Do not fuse the rope end with flame; it's redundant and creates a hard, sharp surface.

Seizings

S eizings are made from mere bits of twine, but they're so strong and secure that they rival Eye Splices. In fact three or four seizings, with no slack in the end or standing part among them, are a sensible alternative to an Eye Splice for stiff old braided line, provided that chafe won't be severe.

An eye seized around a thimble in the middle of a sling means that the sling won't chafe or shift on the hook under load. And a thimble that is seized into an oversized eye is held in very securely, yet can be replaced if it becomes damaged, without cutting the splice.

A seizing starts out like a Braid Whipping, except that instead of burying the end you start binding right away with a kind of Trucker's Hitch. You add a second layer of turns, for extra strength and chafe-resistance, and finish with two frapping turns, taken between the two parts of the line.

Two-Leg Seizing

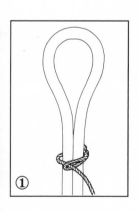

① Splice a small eye into 1 end of an 8-foot length of stout twine (#42 tarred nylon seine twine is a good size to use for seizing 3/8- to 1/2-inch rope.)

Thread the end of the twine through the eye and place it around the middled rope, with the eye pointing left. Tighten the twine around the 2 parts of the rope. If you are seizing a thimble into the rope eye, start the seizing about 1 1/2 inches below the thimble.

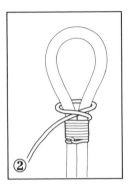

② Begin making tight, even turns upward, against the lay. Haul each turn taut, preferably with a marlingspike. When the seizing is roughly square, form a Half-Hitch with the twine around the rope. Pull this hitch taut.

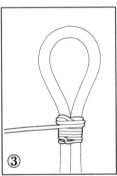

③ Begin a 2nd layer of turns, over the 1st layer (These are called riding turns). Make these a little less tight, so they do not sink down and displace the 1st layer.

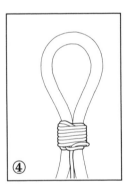

④ When the 1st layer of turns is completely covered, stick the end through the Eye Splice in the end of the twine. Use an awl, large sail needle, or small Fid-O awl to accomplish this. Pull the last turn tight.

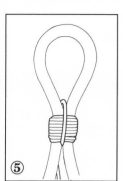

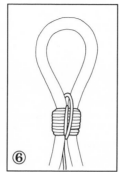

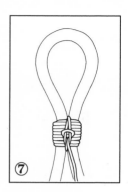

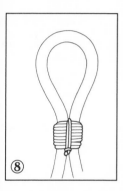

⑤ Turn the seizing over and begin frapping turns: Lead the twine up, through the eye of the rope, down on the far side of the seizing, and back up between the legs of the rope. Haul very taut. This makes the 1st frapping turn.

⑥ Make a 2nd frapping turn, to the right of the first. Haul very taut.

⑦ Make a Flat Knot around the 2 frapping turns: Pass the end under the turn on the left, over both turns, then in under the turn on the right. Haul downward to tighten, and trim the twine close to the Flat Knot.

⑧ The finished seizing.

Four-Leg Seizing

This seizing involves 2 lengths of middled rope. Begin as for a Two-Leg Seizing, but of course wrap around all 4 legs. Finish the frapping turns and pull the Flat Knot down underneath the middle of the seizing. Lead the end up at right angles to the 1st set of frapping turns, and make a 2nd set. Finish with a 2nd Flat Knot.

Shoelaces

EXTRA SECURE

*D*id you know that the bows and ends of a Shoelace Knot properly lie athwartshoe (facing the sides of the feet) rather than fore and aft? The former is a variation on the Square Knot (see page 82), while the latter is a variation on the less secure, less tidy Granny Knot. If you've been tying a Granny Knot, the easiest way to fix it is by reversing the way you tie the initial Overhand Knot.

If you get that part set, you're ready for an ultra-secure, easily made and untied variation for slick shoelaces. When laces won't stay tied, people usually tie a bulky, three-tiered, jam-prone knot, the "Double Knot." The knot here is elegant and secure, and it can be untied simply by pulling on the ends.

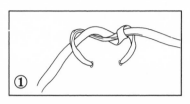

① Begin as for a regular Shoelace Knot, but pass the working end around twice.

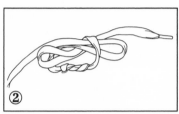

② Make the bow as for a regular Shoelace Knot, but leave a space between the bow and the 1st half of the knot.

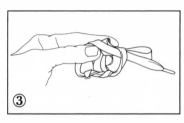

③ Pass an end and its loop through this space, making an extra turn.

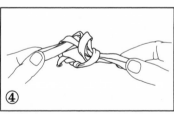

④ Draw up by pulling on the loops.

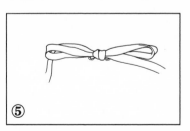

⑤ The finished knot. It can be released by pulling on the ends, as for a regular Shoelace Knot.

CHAPTER TWELVE

FANCY WORK

K nots are tools, but they can also be ornaments with which to adorn handles, wheels, yourself, or anything else you can get string around. This kind of knotting is called Fancy Work.

Old-time sailors came up with some truly byzantine Fancy Work, requiring serious study to decode. But you can make some pretty tricky ornaments yourself, starting with knots you already know.

For example, the Single Constrictor is readily made into an endless braid known as a Turk's Head. And starting with a Lineman's Loop you can make two more Turk's Heads of different proportions. Drawn up very tight, a Turk's Head makes a good grip on a tool handle. Left looser, it's a handsome bracelet.

If you make a whole bunch of Half-Hitches in particular sequences, you'll have a handsome, comfortable-to-grip knot-covering of any length you like. Three patterns of Half-Hitching are shown here.

Fancy Work is satisfying work. Take a break with it now and then when you're weary of things . . . like studying the other knots in this book.

Turk's Head

FROM SINGLE CONSTRICTOR

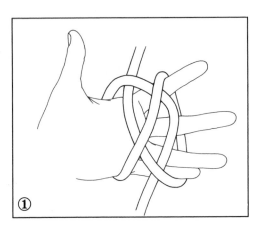

① Tie a Single Constrictor. Arrange it loosely as shown, with the Overhand Knot pulled apart, crossed diagonally by the crossing turn. End is on top, standing part on bottom.

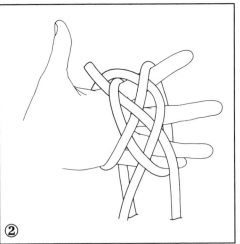

② Lead the end down behind the hand diagonally, towards your fingertips. Lead it up diagonally across the palm of the hand towards your thumb. Tuck it under, over, and under, as shown.

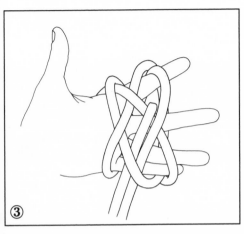

③ Lead the end straight down behind the hand, then thread the end into the knot, right alongside the standing part. This completes the basic structure; it now only remains to double or triple the knot.

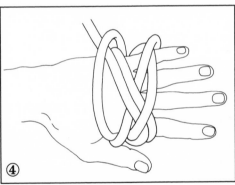

④ Turn the back of your hand towards you. Continue following the standing part with the end. Always keep the end on the same side of the standing part.

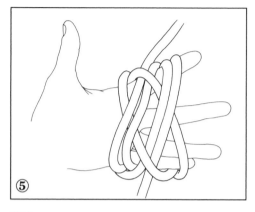

⑤ Turn your palm up again, and continue following the standing part, doubling it, and turning your hand as necessary . . .

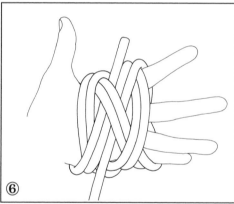

⑥ . . . until end and standing part meet once more under the same turn. This knot is now doubled. If you wish to triple it, simply lead the end around once more, until end and standing part are again under the same turn. Then remove the knot from your hand and place it on its home. Draw up by working the slack out gradually, first by hand, then with the tip of a spike. When the knot is very tight, trim the ends off flush. If you wish to use the knot as a bracelet, fair it up, then glue or stitch the ends under the turn before trimming.

Turk's Head
FROM LINEMAN'S LOOP START

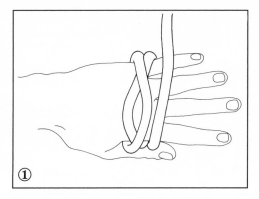

① Make 3 turns around your hand, as though beginning a Single Lineman's Loop. Turn the back of your hand towards you. Move the middle turn under, to the left.

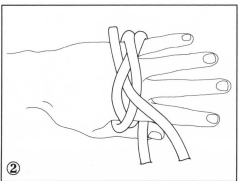

② Pass the end over and under, to the left.

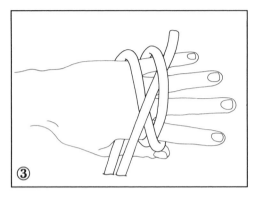

③ Move the original middle turn back to the middle.

④ Pass the end over and under, to the right.

⑤ Move the middle turn once more under, to the left, and pass the end once more over and under, to the left. Double and triple the knot, as for the Turk's Head from Single Constrictor, by paralleling the standing part with the end.

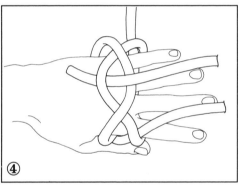

Note: The above directions will produce a knot of 3 leads (a 3-strand braid) and 5 bights (5 scalloped edges on each side of the knot). Moving the middle turn and passing the end twice more will produce a knot of 3 leads and 8 bights. Three more passes beyond that will result in 3 leads and 11 bights, and so on.

If at the commencement of the knot you pass the end over and under first, then move the middle bight under to the right, you will end up with 3 leads and 4 bights. Continued braiding will result in 3 x 7, 3 x 10, etc.

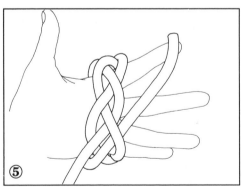

French Hitching

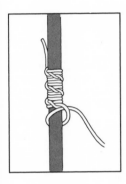

Make a series of Half-Hitches, one on top of the other.
Pull each Hitch taut before proceeding to the next.

St. Mary's Hitching

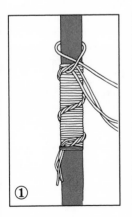

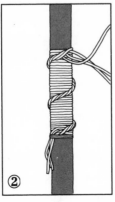

① Constrictor 3 strands of twine at 1 end of the area to be covered. Half-hitch each in turn, always laying the lowest strand over the other

② Carefully fair each Hitch as it is tied. The finished piece should have the appearance of 3-strand rope laid in a spiral over a series of plain turns.

Ringbolt Hitching

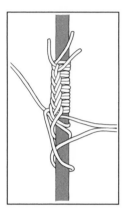

Affix 3 pieces of twine to the hitchee. Hitch 1 piece to the left, the next to the right, the next to the left, and so on. Draw up each Hitch before making the next, and draw up all Hitches evenly, so the "spine" of the hitching stays straight. Cover the ends with Turk's Heads.

CHAPTER THIRTEEN

THE END

Every line has two ends. In general, you put a line to work by attaching one end to a load and leading the other end to your hands. Knotting is primarily concerned with what happens at the load. But we'll close with what happens at your end of the line.

The idea is to make the end of the line bulky, so that you know when you've come to the end of it, and won't let it slip through your hands, and so that even if it does slip through, it will fetch up in a block or fairlead instead of unreeving itself.

The Figure-Eight Knot is the traditional end-of-line knot. It's easy to tie, amply bulky, and quite secure. As a bonus, it makes a useful Loop Knot when tied with the bight—jam-prone but secure.

Make an extra half-turn and you have a Stevedore Knot. When the line is slick, or when a Figure Eight isn't quite big enough, the Stevedore is the oversize, stay-together alternative.

And that's the end of this collection. Assess your ropework needs and study accordingly. It could be that for normal needs you will require only a few of the knots in this handbook. But take a look at the rest, both to prepare yourself for the unusual, and for a perspective on the knots you use.

It could also be that you will undertake a more ambitious relationship with rope. In that case, I hope that this book will provide you with a useful introduction to the art.

Whatever your level of interest, practice *your* knots until they live in your hands, and they will serve you well.

Figure-Eight Knot

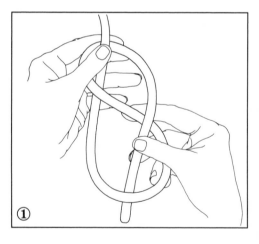

① Form a loop, end in front of standing part. Pass the end behind the standing part, then down through the loop, away from you. Draw up.

② The finished knot.

Figure-Eight Knot
TIED IN THE BIGHT

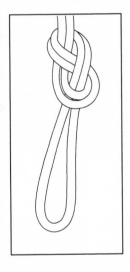

Form a long bight. Tie a Figure-Eight Knot with this bight just as you would with the end. Keep the 2 parts of the line fair and parallel as you draw up.

Stevedore Knot

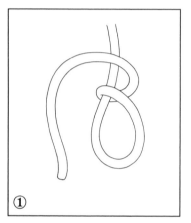

①

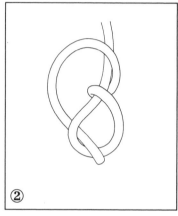

②

③

① Start with a loop, end in front of standing part, as for the Figure-Eight Knot. Make a round turn with the end around the standing part, working away from the loop.

② Drop the end down into the loop, towards you. Draw up.

③ The finished knot.

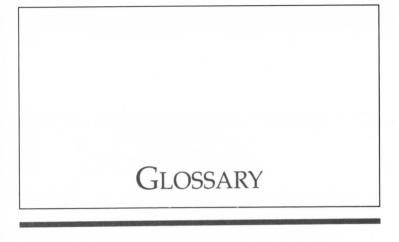

GLOSSARY

Against the lay passed in the opposite direction from that in which the STRANDs twist, but in the same direction of lengthwise travel

Aloft above, overhead

Anchor Rode a length of chain or rope, or a combination of chain and rope, connecting a vessel to its anchor

Athwartships at right angles to a vessel's fore-and-aft plane

Bail (1) a piece of U-shaped hardware fitted to masts and booms, to which STANDING or RUNNING RIGGING is attached. (2) A metal EYE at the head of a BLOCK from which the block is suspended.

Becket (1) the EYE at the end of a LINE. (2) The eye at the base of a BLOCK, to which the standing end of a TACKLE is attached.

Belay (1) to secure a ROPE, usually to a CLEAT or BELAYING PIN. (2) The place at which or fixture to which a LINE is belayed ("One generally coils away from the belay"). (3) The HITCH that forms the belay ("a turn, two figure-eight turns, and a hitch form a secure belay").

Belaying Pin a short pin of wood or metal to which RUNNING RIGGING is secured

Bend a knot that joins two ENDs together

Bight (1) any curved or doubled section of a ROPE. (2) One of the scalloped edges of a Turk's Head Knot, formed by the change of direction of a LEAD.

Binding Knot any knot used to contain or bind objects together

Bitts two sturdy upright posts affixed to the foredeck of a vessel, to which LINES are BELAYed. Bitts are usually rectangular in cross-section.

Block a metal or wooden housing containing a SHEAVE, through which ROPE is led, either to effect a change in direction or to increase mechanical advantage

Block and tackle an arrangement of BLOCKs and ROPE which provides a mechanical advantage. Also known simply as TACKLE.

Bollard two sturdy upright posts, usually of metal and round in cross-section, to which LINES are BELAYed

Boom a SPAR used to extend the foot of a sail

Bosun's Chair a seat to which a HALYARD is attached for hauling a crewmember ALOFT

Braid-over-filament a ROPE construction in which a braided cover surrounds a bundle of parallel FILAMENTs

Brail to bundle a sail against a mast or STAY

Breast line a MOORING line leading at right-angles to a vessel's fore-and-aft dimension

Capsize in knotting, to distort or change structure under load

Carabiner a spring-loaded, oval-shaped SHACKLE

Cast off to remove a LINE from its BELAY

Chafe to rub against the FIBERs of ROPE or canvas so as to wear through them

Chock a metal FAIRLEAD, usually open-topped, set into the deck edge at the bow and stern of a vessel, through which MOORING lines are led

Cleat a piece of two-horned hardware, secured to deck, rigging, or SPAR, to which LINES are BELAYed

Clew an EYE in the aft, lower corner of a sail, to which a SHEET is attached

Coil (1) ROPE made up into a series of TURNs, for stowage. (2) To make such turns.

Come-along a portable wire WINCH

Compound purchase a form of mechanical advantage in which one set of BLOCK

AND TACKLE is affixed to the HAULING PART of a second set of block and tackle

Construction of rope, the manner in which composite YARNs are arranged

Crossed round turn a ROUND TURN in which the second PART of the TURN crosses diagonally over the first part

Deck Stopper a short length of ROPE, anchored to the deck at one end, which is wrapped around the STANDING PART of another LINE to maintain tension on that line while the END is BELAYed

Dock line a heavy LINE, preferably NYLON, used to secure a vessel to dock, pier, or shore

Double block (D) a BLOCK that contains two SHEAVES, usually side by side (see **Fiddle Block**)

Double-braid rope a ROPE construction in which a braided core is surrounded by a braided cover

Double with Becket (DWB) a DOUBLE BLOCK with a BECKET at its base

Draw up to tighten a knot until it is firm enough to avoid slippage or CAPSIZE

End the termination of a LINE. in use, the end that is secured to the load is called the *standing end*, while the end that is BELAYed is called the *working end* or *bitter end*

Eye a LOOP or BIGHT that has been secured by knotting, SEIZING, or SPLICing

Eye Splice a form of Loop Knot made by turning the END back and weaving the STRANDs into the STANDING PART

Fairlead any BLOCK, EYE, ring, or other fixture that changes the LEAD of a LINE, so that the line can be hauled, or will lead to a BELAY, at a favorable angle

Fall the HAULING PART of a TACKLE

Fancy work decorative ropework, which may or may not serve a practical purpose

Fiber the basic component of ROPE; see **YARNs**, **STRANDs**

Fid (1) a tapered hardwood pin used to open the STRANDS of a ROPE in order to SPLICE. (2) A square wooden or metal bar which acts as a through-bolt at the base of a topmast, supporting the topmast at the head of a lower mast.

Fid-and-pusher a two-piece system used to SPLICE DOUBLE-BRAID ROPE; the rope end is inserted in one end of a metal FID, and rope and fid are pushed through the core and cover

Fiddle block a type of DOUBLE BLOCK in which the SHEAVES are set one above the other; the upper sheave is larger than the lower, so that ROPE parts leading from the two sheaves will not CHAFE

Fiddle with Becket (FWB) a FIDDLE BLOCK with a BECKET at its base

Filament in ROPE construction, a fine thread drawn from molten plastic; a "filament rope" is one in which the FIBERs are filaments; see **SPUN**

Filament bundle a bundle of FILAMENTs, sometimes wrapped in a thin tape covering, which forms the core of a BRAID-OVER-FILAMENT ROPE

Foot that side of a sail between TACK and CLEW

Frap to haul sideways on a line in order to increase tension

Gaff a SPAR, set on the after side of a mast, which extends the head of a four-sided (gaff) sail

Gasket a length of ROPE, fixed at one end to the YARD of a square-rigged sail, used to LASH the furled sail to the yard

Half-Hitch a TURN of ROPE taken around an object, then back between the object and the rope's own STANDING PART

Halyard a LINE that lifts an object, particularly sails, vertically

Hank a ring or SHACKLE by which a sail is affixed to a STAY. The hank slides on the stay, allowing the sail to be hoisted and lowered.

Hard-laid of ROPE, tightly twisted or tightly braided

Hauling part that part of a TACKLE which is hauled upon; the FALL

Hawser technically, any heavy ROPE of 1 5/8 inches diameter or more; in practice, any rope heavy enough to tow, MOOR, or anchor with

Head of a coil the top part of a COIL, grasped by one hand while coiling

Heaving line a light LINE, weighted at one end and secured by the other end to the EYE of a MOORING line; the heaving line is thrown ashore and the mooring line is hauled ashore with it

Hemp FIBER made from the plant cannabis sativa. Hemp ROPE is usually tarred for preservation.

Hitch a knot by which a ROPE is secured around an object or around the rope's own STANDING PART

Hockle a distortion in the length of the STANDING PART of a THREE-STRAND ROPE, caused by excessively twisting the rope WITH THE LAY; the STRANDs separate from one another, forming BIGHTS, and the bights begin twisting up around themselves

Hose clamp an adjustable metal band, used to clamp hoses to fittings

In the bight a knot made without PASSing either END; see **WITH THE BIGHT**

Kevlar™ an extremely low-stretch synthetic FIBER, used for HALYARDs and SHEETs aboard racing sail boats

Lanyard a short length of ROPE used to secure objects to one another

Lash to secure objects, in order to prevent shifting, with lengths of ROPE or TWINE

Lashing an arrangement of ROPE or TWINE which secures an object or objects

Lay (1) in stranded ROPE, the tightness of the twist of the STRANDs; thus a rope might be said to have a hard, medium, or soft lay. (2) The direction in which the strands are twisted; see **LEFT-LAID, RIGHT-LAID**.

Lead (1) a LINE's course, from its hauling END, through any BLOCKs, FAIRLEADs, CHOCKs, etc., to its BELAY. (2) The direction in which a line travels in a knot. (3) One of the parts which form the braid of a Turk's Head knot.

Leech the after side of a fore-and-aft sail, or the outer sides of a squaresail

Left-laid stranded ROPE twisted together so that as one sights down the length of the rope, the STRANDs spiral away to the left. A rare CONSTRUCTION.

Line in general, a length of ROPE which has been put to a specific use, such as a HALYARD or SHEET; exceptions in usage include: footrope, bellrope, tiller rope, boltrope, manrope, etc.

Loop (1) a closed or crossed BIGHT. (2) A knotted bight.

Luff the leading edge of a sail

Manila FIBERs of the abaca plant, which grows in the Philippines

Marl to wrap with a series of MARLING HITCHEs

Marling Hitch a TURN of ROPE around an object, then over and under the STANDING PART

Marlingspike a tapered metal FID used to tighten SEIZINGs, SPLICE wire, chip, pry, wedge, and perform various other tasks

Marlingspike Hitch a slipknot, made around the tip of a MARLINGSPIKE, for hauling SEIZINGs and LASHINGs taut

Monkey's Fist a spherical knot, made around a weight, used at the END of a HEAVING LINE

Moor (1) to tie to a dock or buoy. (2) To anchor between two anchors.

Mooring a permanent anchor. A chain attached to it leads to a mooring buoy at the surface. Vessels tie to the buoy.

Nylon a high-strength, elastic, synthetic FIBER. Nylon ROPEs are commonly used as anchor and DOCK LINEs.

On the bight see **IN THE BIGHT**

Palm a sewing device for ROPE, leather, and canvas, which is worn around the hand. It is a flat leather strap with a thumb hole, with a THIMBLE, or "iron," set at the base of the thumb. The butt of the needle is braced in the iron, so that the needle can be pushed through the fabric.

Part a portion of LINE. The inactive bulk of a line is the STANDING PART, the section nearest the END is sometimes referred to as "its own part."

Pass to take a LINE around an object, as in "to pass a TURN around a PIN" or "to pass the END through a THIMBLE"

Pendant a length of ROPE fixed at one end, with a PURCHASE attached to the other end; see **RUNNING BACKSTAY**

Pin see **BELAYING PIN**

Polypropylene the lightest of synthetic FIBERs commonly used to make ROPE. Polypropylene floats, but is subject to CHAFE and deterioration from sunlight.

Preventer a PENDANT or TACKLE which restrains the motion of a mast or BOOM

Purchase in rigging, a means to increase power or force by the use of BLOCKS, WINCHES, levers, or gears

Race in BLOCKS, a groove around the axle hole of the SHEAVE, in which bearings roll

Reeve (past tense, rove) (1) to pass the end of a ROPE through a hole. (2) To lace a set of BLOCKS together.

Rig (1) to fit out with SPARs, ROPE, STAYs, and sails. (2) The configurations of SPARs, SHROUDs, STAYs, and sails that determine a sailing vessel's type (i.e., cutter rig, ketch rig, schooner rig, etc.).

Rigger one who works with RIGGING

Rigging in a sailing vessel, any wire, ROPE, or chain that supports, SPARs (STANDING RIGGING), or that raises, lowers, or trims sails (RUNNING RIGGING)

Rigging, running RIGGING used to move things

Rigging, standing the fixed RIGGING, usually of wire, that holds mast and bowsprit in place

Right-laid stranded ROPE twisted together so that as one sights down the length of the rope, the STRANDS spiral away to the right. Nearly all currently-produced STRANDED ROPE is right-laid three-strand.

Ringbolt hitching   a form of decorative HITCHing especially useful for covering curved objects. In the days of large HEMP ANCHOR RODES the rode at anchor was LASHED to ringbolts secured to the deck. Ringbolt hitching was used to prevent CHAFE.

Rope   a flexible cord of twisted or braided CONSTRUCTION. In general usage, cordage of less than 1/4-inch diameter is referred to as TWINE, lashing line, or small stuff.

Rope clutch   a mechanical DECK STOPPER in which shaped jaws clamp on the ROPE

Round Turn   two TURNs around an object

Run   of ROPE, to travel unimpeded for quick lowering of sails. A HALYARD is CAST OFF and let run.

Running backstay   a type of PREVENTER STAY for a mast, comprising a PENDANT, usually of wire, which leads from the mast to near deck, and a PURCHASE or ROPE tail which is BELAYed on deck

Sail Tie   a short piece of webbing or ROPE used to secure a furled sail

Samson post   a sturdy, upright post, affixed to the foredeck of a vessel, to which LINEs are BELAYed; see **BITTS**

Seaway   a sea route

Seize   to bind two or more PARTs of ROPE together with TWINE

Seizing   a type of LASHING, made with TWINE or wire, that binds together two or more PARTs of ROPE or wire rope

Self-tailing winch   a WINCH with a grooved cap fitted to its top which makes hand tailing unnecessary; see **TAILING**

Selvagee   a curcular STROP used as a STOPPER and SLING

Set up   to tighten STANDING RIGGING; to TUNE

Shackle   a metal fitting with a pinned or hinged opening, for attaching rigging to SPARs, sails, hull, or to other rigging

Sheave   the grooved wheel of a BLOCK

Sheer pole   a horizontal wooden or metal truss, bolted or SEIZEd to the lower SHROUDs, just above the TURNBUCKLEs. Originally meant to keep the shrouds from untwisting when set up, sheer poles in these days of twist-resistant wire more often serve as racks for BELAYING PINs.

Sheet   a LINE that controls the ATHWARTSHIPS travel of a sail

Sheet-lead block   a deck BLOCK that directs the LEAD of the SHEET at an appropriate angle from the CLEW to an appropriate angle to the WINCH

Shroud   a wire that provides lateral support to a mast

Single block (S)   a BLOCK with one SHEAVE and no BECKET

Single with becket (SWB)   a SINGLE BLOCK with a BECKET at its base

Sissy bars   metal frames, bolted to the deck on either side of mast, to provide crewmembers with something to brace themselves against, and tether themselves to, while working at the mast

Sling   a ROPE, wire, or chain strap, attached to an object for the purpose of hoisting it. The sling is in turn attached to a HALYARD.

Snap shackle   a hinged SHACKLE, held closed by a spring-mounted piston

Snotter   the PENDANT or PURCHASE that holds the butt of the SPRIT close to the mast in sprit-rigged craft

Soft eye   a THIMBLEless EYE; a RIGGING eye that encircles a mast or BOOM

Soft-laid   of ROPE, slackly-twisted or braided

Spar   a wooden or metal RIGGING support, including all masts, YARDs, GAFFs, SPRITs, SPREADERs, etc.

Spiral lashing   a LASHING that secures a sail to a mast or BOOM with a continuous spiral of LINE

Splice   (1) a BEND or EYE formed by interweaving the STRANDs of ROPE or ropes. (2) To create such a bend or eye.

Spreader   a strut that deflects the LEAD of a piece of STANDING RIGGING, in order to reduce the compression load on the SPAR to which the rigging attaches, and/or to stabilize the spar

Spring   of MOORING to a dock, to locate a vessel fore and aft with forward- and aft-leading LINES. The lines usually lead from the vessel's amidships area, to minimize dock length used.

Spring line   a MOORING line used to SPRING a vessel

Sprit   the SPAR that stretches diagonally across a four-sided fore-and-aft sail to support the peak

Spun   of cordage, a CONSTRUCTION in which the FIBERs are short pieces (as opposed to filament fibers), that are spun together to form the YARNs

Stanchions the upright supports set at intervals along the sides of a vessel's deck, to carry the guardrail or lifelines

Standing part the inactive part of a LINE

Stay a wire that provides a mast with fore-and-aft support. Stays are named according to their function, hence backstay, jibstay, etc.

Stays'l a fore-and-aft sail, usually triangular, which is set by being HANKed to a STAY or set parallel to it.

Stick to TUCK

Stop a light LASHING that secures a sail or COIL of ROPE

Stopped said of a COIL of ROPE or a sail that is bound by a series of short lengths of TWINE

Stopper (1) to apply STOPS to a COIL of ROPE or a sail. (2) To apply a DECK STOPPER to a piece of RUNNING RIGGING.

Stopper knot a knot in the end of a LINE that prevents it from unREEVing through a BLOCK or FAIRLEAD

Strand two or more YARNs twisted together

Stranded rope ROPE made by twisting STRANDs about each other

Strop (1) a ROPE, SPLICEd into a circle, that fits around a BLOCK or SPAR. Some strops have a tail by which the block can be attached to the rigging. (2) To SEIZE a rope around a block or spar.

Surge to slack away a LINE around a PIN, CLEAT, or post

Sweat to haul sideways on a LINE, usually a HALYARD, to gain more tension than is possible with a pull parallel with the LEAD of the line. Sweating is a form of FRAPping.

Sweat hook a hook that is fixed to the deck below a HALYARD's PIN or CLEAT. The halyard is led down through the hook, which is U-shaped in contour, then up to the pin, making it easier to SWEAT on the LINE.

Swivel a pivoting link, such as is found in a SWIVEL BLOCK, that permits free turning of items attached to it

Swivel block a BLOCK with an integral SWIVEL in its BAIL, so that the block may pivot horizontally as the LEAD to the block changes

Tack the lower forward corner of a fore-and-aft sail

Tackle see BLOCK AND TACKLE

Tack line a PURCHASE, used instead of a TACK PENDANT, for adjusting LUFF tension

Tack pendant a short PENDANT running from a deck fitting to the TACK, to set the height to which the sail is hoisted

Tail to maintain tension on a LINE as it leads from a BELAY or WINCH

Take a turn to put a TURN on a BELAYING fixture, in order to control a load by TAILing

Thimble a circular or teardrop-shaped collar, of plastic or metal, around which ROPE or wire rope is bent to be EYE SPLICEd. In use, the thimble prevents CHAFE and deformation of the rope.

Throat (1) of a four-sided, fore-and-aft sail, the upper foremost corner. (2) of an EYE SPLICE, the point at which the two legs of the EYE meet.

Toggle for ROPE, a removable metal or wooden pin, used to effect temporary, quickly released BENDs or LOOPs

Tuck to pass a STRAND between other strands, particularly in forming an EYE SPLICE

Tune to set up the STANDING RIGGING of a sailing vessel so that the relative tension of the SHROUDs and STAYs produces optimal mast support and sail shape

Turn one round of a LINE around an object

Turnbuckle an adjustable, double-threaded fitting, by which rigging is set up

Turning block a BLOCK that redirects the LEAD of a LINE

Twine stout string, usually waxed or tarred, made of two or more twisted STRANDs

Vang a PURCHASE or PENDANT that prevents travel of a BOOM or GAFF

Whipping a TWINE binding on the END of a LINE which prevents the STRANDs from ravelling

Winch a rotating barrel, hand or power driven, around which ROPE is wrapped, to gain tension

With the bight tied using a BIGHT, its two sides pressed together as though it were an END

With the lay passed in the same direction as that in which the STRANDs twist, in the same direction of travel

Yard a wooden or metal SPAR, crossing a mast, from which a sail or sails are hung

Yarn a substructure of ROPE, made by twisting FIBERs together. Yarns are in turn twisted together into STRANDs, and strands into rope.

CHARTS

Relative weights and strengths of synthetic rope materials

Nominal Size		Nylon		Dacron		Multiline II		Polypropylene	
Dia	Circ.	Weight Lbs/ 100 ft.	Average Tensile Strength	Weight Lbs/ 100 ft.	Average Tensile Strength	Weight Lbs/ 100 ft.	Average Tensile Strength	Weight Lbs/ 100 ft.	Average Tensile Strength
3/16"	9/16"	1.0	1.2	1.2	1.2	—	—	.7	.856
1/4"	3/4"	1.5	2.	2.0	2.	—	—	1.2	1.35
5/16"	1"	2.5	3.	3.1	3.	2.5	2.2	1.8	2.05
3/8"	1-1/8"	3.5	4.4	4.5	4.4	3.6	3.2	2.8	2.9
7/16"	1-1/4"	5.0	5.9	6.2	5.9	5.0	4.1	3.8	3.8
1/2"	1-1/2"	6.5	7.5	8.0	7.5	6.5	5.8	4.7	4.7
9/16"	1-3/4"	8.2	9.4	10.2	8.9	8.0	6.6	6.1	5.45
5/8"	2"	10.5	12.2	13.0	11.7	9.5	8.2	7.5	7.
3/4"	2-1/4"	14.5	16.7	17.5	14.7	12.5	10.8	10.7	9.4
7/8"	2-3/4"	20.0	23.5	25.0	21.1	18.0	15.5	15.0	13.
1"	3"	26.4	29.4	30.4	25.8	21.8	18.7	18.0	15.7

* Average tensile strengths listed in thousands of pounds (1.5 = 1500)

Relative rope elasticities

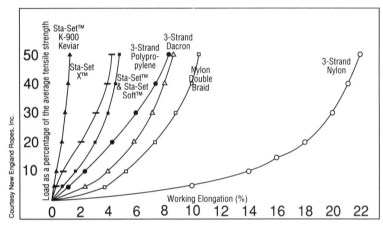

Courtesy New England Ropes, Inc.

190

INDEX

192